Joseph George Cumming

Antiquitates Manniae

A Collection of Memoirs on the Antiquities of the Isle of Man

Joseph George Cumming

Antiquitates Manniae
A Collection of Memoirs on the Antiquities of the Isle of Man

ISBN/EAN: 9783337412999

Printed in Europe, USA, Canada, Australia, Japan

Cover: Foto ©ninafisch / pixelio.de

More available books at **www.hansebooks.com**

The Manx Society,

ESTABLISHED IN THE YEAR

MDCCCLVIII.

VOL. XV.

DOUGLAS, ISLE OF MAN:
PRINTED FOR THE MANX SOCIETY.
MDCCCLXVIII.

N.B.—Members at a distance are (as heretofore) requested to acknowledge their Copies to the Honorary Secretary and Treasurer, Mr. PAUL BRIDSON, 6, Woodbourne Square, to whom also their Subscriptions can be remitted.

ANTIQUITATES MANNIÆ:

OR, A

COLLECTION OF MEMOIRS

ON THE

ANTIQUITIES OF THE ISLE OF MAN.

Edited for the Manx Society

BY THE

REV. J. G. CUMMING, M.A., F.G.S.,

INCUMBENT OF ST. JOHN'S, BETHNAL GREEN, LONDON; LATE WARDEN OF QUEEN'S COLLEGE,
BIRMINGHAM; FORMERLY VICE-PRINCIPAL OF KING WILLIAM'S COLLEGE,
ISLE OF MAN.

LONDON:
PRINTED FOR THE MANX SOCIETY.
MDCCCLXVIII.

T. RICHARDS, PRINTER, 37, GREAT QUEEN STREET, W.C.

PREFACE.

THE Manx Society was established *primarily* for the publication of old and scarce books, manuscripts, and documents, pertaining to the history of the Isle of Man, and its volumes, previous to this, have strictly followed out that design. But at the meeting of the Cambrian Archæological Association at Douglas in the year 1865, it was seen that the more ancient history of the island would be greatly elucidated by the consideration of the very many remarkable relics left behind them by its former inhabitants, in buildings, tumuli, kistvaens, bauta stones, and runic monuments, both inscribed and uninscribed. Hence the Council of the Manx Society considered that it would much conduce to the interest and usefulness of its publications if they included in them the various Memoirs on the Antiquities of the Isle which were read at that meeting, together with others of a similar character. The very ready and most generous consent of the Council of the Cambrian

Archæological Association was therefore obtained for
the republication of the Memoirs on Manx Antiquities
which appeared in the *Archæologia Cambrensis* during
the years 1866-7, and the further most liberal use was
acquired of the plates of the engravings and the blocks
of the woodcuts illustrating the Memoirs in that
Journal.

To the Cambrian Archæological Association the Council of the Manx Society desire to return their deepest
acknowledgments for their generosity.

The present volume consists wholly of the Memoirs
read at the Douglas Meeting, with such emendations
and additions as the various authors of them have
thought desirable, amongst which may be mentioned
some new and interesting readings and interpretations
of the runic inscriptions by myself, and the fuller account of the Ancient Churches of Man by Dr. Oliver.

Manx antiquities are by no means exhausted in these
Memoirs. The Runic Monuments, of which only a few
examples are given in this volume, open up a wide
field for investigation. Excavations have recently been
made, during the progress of the Ordnance Trigono-
metrical Survey of the Isle of Man, in some of the
ancient Tumuli and amidst the Stone Circles, which
throw much light upon the ancient modes of sepulture
and the habits and character of the Aborigines of the
Island.

The Coins and Seals also which have been preserved, deserve a more careful examination than has hitherto been bestowed upon them.

Hence, a Second volume of the Antiquities of the Island is under the consideration of the Council of the Manx Society, and may probably be expected at an early date.

. It is hoped that the present volume, with its ample and well-executed illustrations, may be the means of awakening a deeper interest in the Isle of Man, where the relics of the past have been guarded with a more religious veneration than has been accorded to them by the people of the surrounding British Isles. The isolation of the country has no doubt in some degree contributed to this result ; but credit must also be given to the deep religious feeling of Manxmen, not altogether unalloyed with superstition, which has led them to abstain from the destruction of the monuments of the dead, and of the places where their forefathers worshipped. They reap their reward in the materials which they have thus preserved to the Antiquary for elucidating their earlier history.

The Editor desires to acknowledge the deep obligation under which he lies to the Rev. E. L. Barnwell and Dr. Oliver, for the assistance which they have afforded him in passing these sheets through the press.

The publication must, in reality, be considered as under a joint editorship. One emendation in the text of these papers it seems desirable to make. It would perhaps have been better to have named, on page 34, Maelmore as a *"Royal personage"* or *"Princess"*, than as a probable *" Queen* of Man".

J. G. CUMMING.

St. John's Parsonage, Victoria Park Square, London, N.E.
June 1st, 1868.

TABLE OF CONTENTS.

PAGE

1. On the Ornamentation of the Runic Monuments in the Isle of Man . . Rev. J. G. Cumming, M.A., F.G.S. 1
2. On some more Recently Discovered Scandinavian Crosses in the Isle of Man . . . . . Rev. J. G. Cumming 13
3. The Runic Inscriptions of the Isle of Man.
   Rev. J. G. Cumming 19
4. Rushen Abbey in the Isle of Man . Rev. J. G. Cumming 36
5. Robert the Brus before Rushen Castle.
   Rev. J. G. Cumming 56
6. Ancient Churches of the Isle of Man prior to the Middle Ages . . . . J. R. Oliver, Esq., M.D. 60
7. Notes on the Stone Monuments in the Isle of Man.
   Rev. E. L. Barnwell, M.A. 92
8. Church Furniture in Malew Church, Isle of Man.
   Rev. E. L. Barnwell, M.A. 107
9. On Certain Bronze Implements, Isle of Man.
   Rev. E. L. Barnwell, M.A. 111
10. Circle on "The Mull", Isle of Man.
    J. M. Jeffcott, Esq., H.K. 113
11. Mananan Mac Lir: His Mythic Connection with the Isle of Man . . . . Richard R. Brash, Esq., M.R.I.A. 119

LIST OF PLATES.

Ornamentation of Manx Runic Crosses. Plates I and II . 8
Fragment of an Inscribed Cross in Braddan Churchyard . . 12
Cross in Kirk Maughold Churchyard 14
Cross at Kirk Maughold, Isle of Man, formerly built into the Western Gable of the Church 16
Cross in Kirk Maughold Churchyard, and Cross in a Treen Chapel near Ballaglass, Kirk Maughold, Isle of Man . 18
Runic Inscriptions on Crosses in the Isle of Man . . . 23

viii CONTENTS.

Ruined Tower, Rushen Abbey, Isle of Man 40
Crossag Bridge, near Rushen Abbey 42
Ballingan Treen Church and Enclosure, Kirk Marown . . 78
Manx Cabbal of the Fifth Century 80
The Keeill of the Sixth Century 82
Doorway, Ballaquinney Treen Church 84
Treen Church of the Eighth Century 86
St. Luke's Chapel, and Burial-ground of the Danish Kings,
    Cronk-na-Irey-Lhaa 90
Plan of Oatlands Circle, Isle of Man 96
Oatlands Circle, Isle of Man 96
Stone with Cup Markings, Oatlands Circle 96
Stone Avenue, Poor Town, near Peel, Isle of Man . . 96
Circle on Mull Hill, Isle of Man 96
Kistvaen near St. John's, Tynwald Mount, Isle of Man . . 96
Beads, Rock Crystal and Ornaments found in a Kistvaen near
    St. John's, Tynwald Mount, Isle of Man 103
Paten, Kirk Malew, Isle of Man 106
Portion of Staff Covered with Brass, and Processional Lantern
    Top, Malew Church 108
Chalice from the Parish of Jurby, Isle of Man . . . 110

LIST OF WOODCUTS IN THE TEXT.

Chamfered Arch in Rushen Abbey 39
Single-Light Window, Rushen Abbey 40
Stone Font, Keeill Pharic 83
Stone Font, St. Lingan's 84
Doorway, Keeill St. Lingan 85
Interior Walling of Ballaquinney Treen Keeill . . . 86
Rock at Ballamona 95
Plan of Circle on Mull Hill 101
Crucifix, Kirk Malew 108
Mould for Bronze Implements 112
Plan of Circle on the Mull 114

MANX ANTIQUITIES.

ON THE ORNAMENTATION OF THE RUNIC
MONUMENTS IN THE ISLE OF MAN.

BY THE REV. J. G. CUMMING, M.A., F.G.S.

THE Northmen, during their occupation of the Isle of Man, from A.D. 888 to A.D. 1270, a period of nearly four hundred years, passed from a state of heathenism into Christianity. This change is marked by the character of the sepulchral monuments which they have left behind them.

The barrows and bauta stones, and perhaps some of the stone circles, indicate their earlier religious condition; their later is marked by the Runic Crosses, Peel Cathedral, Rushen Abbey, the Nunnery of St. Bridget at Douglas, and the Friary at Bechmaken in Arbory.

The Runic crosses are probably the earliest *Christian* remains of this people, and they are by far the most numerous, not less than thirty-eight having been discovered and described, of which nineteen, if not more, have on them inscriptions in Runic characters.

From the nature of the ornamentation upon those which are inscribed with Runes, we are enabled to determine by comparison that other crosses, not inscribed, are of the same age with them. For though the peculiar ornamentation which has received the name of knot-work is common to English, Irish, and Scotch crosses, as well as to the Manx, there are certain remarkable varieties of design and workmanship on the crosses

B

of the Isle of Man, which readily distinguish them from all
others, and mark them as truly *sui generis*. The Manx crosses
have, as far as I know, no exact counterparts elsewhere.

This will readily be seen by any one who will take the
trouble to lay the plates of my *Runic and other Monumental
Remains of the Isle of Man* alongside of the splendid *Palæo-
graphia Sacra Pictoria* of Mr. Westwood; or the beautiful
work of the late Mr. Chalmers, *The Sculptured Stones of Angus
and Fyfe;* or the more extensive collection of *Scottish Sculptured Stones*, printed for the Spalding Club; or Mr. Henry
O'Neil's magnificent book on the *Most Interesting of the Crosses
of Ireland;* or Mr. Graham's deeply interesting work, the
Antiquities of Iona.

Before directing attention to the peculiar ornamentation of
the Manx Crosses, it may be well to offer a few remarks upon
knot-work itself.

The term knot-work has been applied to a species of ornament of great beauty and variety which is met with in MSS.
and articles of vertu, and of monuments and architecture of
the Middle Ages.

The MS. of the Gospels (known by the name of St. Chad's
MS.) in the library of Lichfield Cathedral, by some presumed
to be of the early part of the eighth century, has various rich
illuminations in which this style of ornament prevails. The
Gospels of Mac Durnan, of Lindisfarne, of Mac Regol, and at
St. Gall, and the famous Book of Kells, are all remarkable for
the intricacy and rich variety of this kind of work.

Good examples of this species of ornamentation are to be
met with in Norman architecture, as, amongst many others, in
Lichfield Cathedral; in the parish church of Tutbury; and in the
Church of St. Peter's, Northampton. But it is on monumental
crosses that patterns of this peculiar decoration seem most
largely to prevail.

Starting from the form of a simple cord or *strap*, then of
two or more cords or *straps* intertwined, it has passed (as I

conceive) into floriation, assuming the forms of interlacing boughs and foliage, and at all times has had a tendency to zoomorphism, transforming itself into grotesque figures of intertwining monstrous animals, more especially of dogs, birds, fishes, and serpents.

There is probably no species of decoration admitting of greater variety than this, and hardly any which adapts itself so readily to every sort of work in wood, stone, or metal, and to the illumination of every kind of writing.

It will be seen that, in reference to this species of ornamentation, I am quite in favour of a theory of development; and I express my adoption of such a theory in order to free myself from the suspicion of attempting to settle the dispute as to whether Britons, Anglo-Saxons, Northmen, the Irish, or the Scotch should lay claim to priority in the use of this sort of decoration in works of art.

I hold that the artists of each of these nations may have wrought quite independently of each other in this kind of work. I have even seen examples of Chinese knot-work not greatly differing from some in the Isle of Man. Starting from the simplest form of a rope common to every people, they might develope that form according to their characteristic national tastes. So that even if it should be determined (which, I believe, it cannot be) that any one race had adopted such ornamentation at an earlier period than others, it by no means necessarily follows that those who subsequently used it were mere copyists of earlier works. I have sometimes been told that the Manx crosses are but bad attempts at imitating Irish or Scotch works of art. Now, whatever may be the antiquity of the *MSS.* in which the same species of ornament occurs as that upon *some* of the Manx crosses, I am quite sure that it has yet to be shewn that any of the *crosses* bearing such ornament either in Ireland or Scotland, are earlier than those in the Isle of Man. We have also some varieties of ornamentation on the Manx crosses (and those of the most beautiful design),

which have no counterpart on either the Irish or Scotch monumental remains.   And it would be quite as easy to suppose
that the Irish and Scotch obtained their designs from the
Manx artists as that the latter were but imitators of what they
had seen in Ireland or Scotland.   I say nothing of the finish or
workmanship on the crosses of the respective countries, because I believe that the material which was wrought upon had
much to do with the finish of the work.   The clay schists of
the Isle of Man, almost the only material of which the Manx
crosses are made, are but ill adapted for carving, and do not
admit of a polish; and, further, they very readily yield to the
action of the weather.

   That we find these crosses, which are seven or eight hundred
years old, retaining as much of their original decoration as
they do, must be attributed to the circumstance that after an
exposure of from two to three hundred years, they were used
as material for the erection of ecclesiastical buildings, instances
of which may be seen now in the Cathedral of Peel and in a
Treen Chapel in Jurby, the former building being of the date
of the thirteenth century.   The majority of the Manx crosses
have been discovered within the last fifty years in pulling
down the old churches in the north of the island and erecting
new ones.   These crosses were figured and described by myself in 1857 in my work on the *Runic and other Monumental
Remains of the Isle of Man*, and the references in this memoir
are to the figures in that work.

   To come to the consideration of the knot-work on the Manx
crosses, I observe that a cord or rope suggests itself very
readily as an ornament to any maritime people, such as those
amongst whom knot-work prevailed.   It may be allowed that a
plain *strap* would equally serve the same purpose; and in flat
work, such as the illumination of MSS., we can readily conceive that such an element in ornamentation would suggest itself.   But in raised work, such as carving on stone, the more
substantial form of the rope would form the ground-work of
the decoration.

Such a simple ornament is found on the Manx crosses as a border to the other devices carved upon the stone. I may instance the well-known so-called Dragon crosses in Braddan churchyard, the Niel Lumgun cross at Kirk Michael, and the fragment found at the old chapel in the Calf of Man. In the last case the cord forms also a portion of the decoration. Figures I and II are reduced from rubbings of the Braddan crosses.

This straight cord would next become waved, and, by being made to return upon itself, would form the *fret* which in various forms occurs upon works of art of all ages. This decoration in the forms so constantly used elsewhere, is not to be found on the Manx crosses, though an approximation to a fret-like appearance is produced on some of them by drawing the lines which divide the strands of a simple cord, or of two cords twisted together, somewhat thick. This character is seen in figure II, which is copied from the *Oter* Dragon cross at Kirk Braddan. The same form occurs also on the large Joalf cross at Kirk Michael, on the top of the large cross at the gates of the churchyard of Kirk Maughold, and on the cross taken from the bell turret of Kirk Maughold, and described in the next memoir.

The mystic *Tau* pattern (see figure IV) so copiously used on monuments, crosses, architecture, and MSS. of all ages, was very largely employed also by the Manx artists on the Runic crosses. We find it on the Ufeig cross at Kirk Andreas, the Thorlaf cross at Ballaugh, the cross in the Treen Chapel at Jurby, on fragments in the churchyard wall at Kirk Michael, and on a fragment in the garden of the vicarage at Jurby.

Again, the C pattern and a spiral appearance were produced by a still further involution of the simple cord, as in figures V and XXX, taken from the Niel Lumgun cross at Kirk Michael. In MSS. this has been largely used, as may be seen in Mr. Westwood's paper on "Early British, Anglo-Saxon, and Irish Ornamentation", in the fortieth part of the *Archæological*

Journal, December 1853. It is also well known in Greek architecture. On the Manx Runic monuments it occurs in its most elaborate forms, both as a border and as scroll-work in connection with the limbs of animals. This is well seen on the fragment of the Dog cross in the garden at Kirk Conchan, on the large cross (uninscribed) at Kirk Maughold, on the Oter Cross at Braddan, on the large Joalf cross at Kirk Michael, on the Sandulf cross at Kirk Andreas, but more remarkably on the Weasel cross in the churchyard of Kirk Conchan.

In this latter cross we have it both for a continuous bordering, and for terminations to straight cords, and also as a separation of the limbs of monstrous animals, in the form of the letter **S** and in the *Gammadion* at the foot of the cross. Figures v, xxii, xxiii, and xxx, are taken from this cross.

Allied to the **T** and **C** patterns was the **Z** pattern (figure iii), of which we have one single instance in the Isle of Man. It occurs on the large cross at Kirk Maughold church gates, which has an aspect quite foreign to the works of the Scandinavian artists in the island. Indeed, all the crosses found at Kirk Maughold have somewhat of a foreign aspect; they are rather Scotch than Manx. Is this circumstance in any way connected with the fact that the church and churchyard of Kirk Maughold (covering three acres) were set apart in ancient times as a Sanctuary?

By causing the simple cord to assume a waved form and then to return and wrap over itself, or by taking two cords and causing them to involve each other at regular intervals, we obtain the simplest form of the guilloche, figure vi, an interlacement well known and very largely used in architecture. Examples of this occur on the Ufeig cross at Kirk Andreas, the Thorlaf cross at Ballaugh, and on fragments at Kirk Michael and Jurby.

It is in this guilloche that we have the real element of knotwork, and the Manx artists having once got hold of this element, wrought it out into a multitude of most elegant forms, many of which I do not remember to have noticed elsewhere. Take, for example, figures VII, VIII, and IX, which are evident developments of the idea, and which are taken from the Malbrigd cross at Kirk Michael, the Thorlaf cross at Ballaugh, and the fragment of Ro's cross in the garden of the vicarage, Jurby.

When once this interlacement or knot-work was effected either by the overlap or splitting up of the strands of a simple rope, it was easy by the multiplication of the cords or strands to originate that endless variety of ornamentation which we see in monuments and works of art of all countries, and most elaborately brought out on the crosses in the Isle of Man.

As to the arrangement of the knot-work, I may here observe that, generally speaking, on Irish monuments or on those which are all presumed to have an Irish origin, the knot-work runs in the form of panels.

On the other hand, in the Manx specimens of the oldest type, the original idea of lengthened and continuous chain work rather prevails. The nearest approach in the Manx crosses to the Irish or Scottish panel work is to be found on the Niel Lumgun cross at Kirk Michael, which, in other respects also differs from the ordinary Manx type; for instance, the runes are of a different form; and, according to Professor Münch, of a later date; the dialect of the inscription is different, and the names occurring in it (such as Niel and Dugald) have rather a Celtic than Norse look. There is a tendency towards this panel-work in the large uninscribed cross at Kirk Maughold church gate, which, as I have before observed, has also a foreign aspect, and one side of the Oter cross at Braddan has two panels containing interlacements. Another cross taken from the bell-turret of Kirk Maughold twelve years ago, and figured and described in the memoir subsequent to this, has also such panel work.

Returning to the consideration of these interlacements or knot-work, we find that the Manx artists made a very easy addition to the ornamentation afforded by the simple guilloche by increasing the number of cords.

A double guilloche was formed by the involution of four cords, as. in figure xi, copied from the Malew cross in the Museum of King William's College, the same pattern being found in the Sandulf cross at Andreas. And, in like manner, by the involution of four cords, we obtain the beautiful figure-of-8 design (see figure xii), which is seen on the fragment of the cross at Kirk Conchan, which I have named the Dog cross, and the rich ornamentation (see figure x) copied from Ro's cross at the vicarage, Jurby.

A very remarkable development of the guilloche, which I have hardly noticed elsewhere, occurs abundantly on crosses in the Isle of Man, to which I would give the name of *ring-work*.

It consists in binding together by an intertwining ring the overlaps of the cord or cords forming the guilloche, as in figures iv and xv, the latter taken from the Ufeig cross at Kirk Andreas.

It occurs on all those crosses the workmanship of which I am inclined to attribute to Gaut Björnson, whose name is given as a cross maker in the inscription on that erected by Malbrigd the son of Athakan Smith, which stands at the churchyard gate of Kirk Michael, as well as in that on the Ufeig cross.

The passage from knot-work to ring-work seems in one instance on the Manx crosses to have been made by accident rather than by design. I refer to the case of knot-work ornamentation on the face of the tall uninscribed cross at the west gate of Braddan churchyard, where, in order to complete the figure in the corner at the top of the cross, the last overlap of the cord forming the knot-work is bound together by a single ring which fills up the vacancy which would otherwise occur, and produces uniformity of appearance. This portion of ornament is given in figure xiii.

The ring being thus once adopted, wide scope for ingenuity was afforded in its arrangement, form, and decoration.

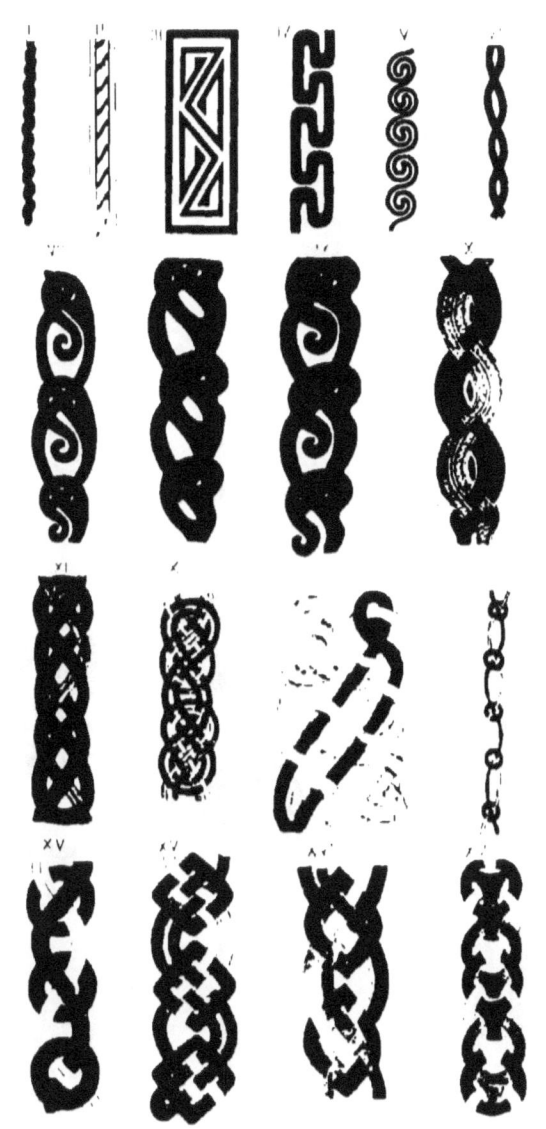

J G Cumming delt   J H St Ives sc

Ornamentation of Manx Runic Crosses

Sometimes the rings were distant and small, as in the beautiful fragment of the cross on the churchyard wall at Kirk Michael (figure xiv). In other cases, the ring was large and either square or lozenge-shaped, as in Joalf's cross at Kirk Michael (figure xvi), where four cords are bound together by a large square ring, and on the fragment of Svig's cross on the churchyard wall of Kirk Michael, where four cords, partly plain, partly pelleted, are bound together by a pelleted lozenge-shaped ring (figure xvii).

This *ring-work* has assumed a variety of configurations, and assists largely in the decoration of the Manx crosses. One of the most beautiful is that given in figure xxv, taken from the large uninscribed cross at Braddan, where it forms a circle or glory surrounding a cruciform pattern of knot-work.

There is, however, one pattern of this ring-work which demands particular attention as a very distinguishing feature in the ornamentation of the Manx crosses. It is the *chain ring-work* displayed in figure xviii, which is so rare elsewhere, if it occur at all, that we may safely claim it as of genuine Manx origin. It certainly does not occur on Irish or Scotch crosses. They have nothing in knot-work comparable to it.

I believe the author of it to have been Gaut Björnson himself. We have it on the Malbrigd cross at Kirk Michael, of which he undoubtedly was the carver. It is on the Thorlaf cross at Ballaugh, the Inosruir cross at St. John's, the Svig cross at Kirk Michael, the inscribed fragment in the churchyard wall of Kirk Michael, the name on which cannot be determined, and on the Ufeig cross at Andreas which is certainly the work of Gaut.

It is so extremely beautiful in its character that we cannot feel at all surprised that it was adopted and applied in a peculiar form upon that cross of Niel Lumgun at Kirk Michael, which I have before pointed out as being of a later date and more foreign aspect.

It is this singular ornament on that cross, together with the

runes, which, to my mind, appropriates it to the Scandinavian
artists of the Isle of Man, notwithstanding its variation from
the general style of Manx crosses and the indications of a
Celtic connection.   The designer of that cross may have seen
Scotch or Irish crosses, if they existed at that time, with knot-
work on them ; but he has indubitably put a Manx stamp
upon it.   The ornament I have alluded to on this cross is given
in figure xxvi.

There are several glories formed of knot-work on the Manx
crosses, as, for instance, those of figures xxv, xxvii, xxix, and
xxxi, but there are none producing so pleasing an effect as this.

I may here observe that the glory seems to have been considered an almost necessary accompaniment to the cross in all
the Manx examples, the only exception appearing to be Ro's
cross at Jurby; but even in this, the ring binding the knot-
work in the head compartment of the cross may be considered
as representing it.   The tall cross, near a cow-shed, at the
cross-roads in Kirk Christ's, Rushen, is too imperfect to determine whether this ornament *did or did not* exist upon it.

I would here notice that the intersection of the strands in
the rope or of the two cords forming the guilloche, bound together by a lozenge-shaped ring, suggested the notion also of
lozenge-shaped pellets *upon* the rope itself, ultimately assuming
the form even of rounded pellets, and giving rise also to the
idea of scale-covered fishes or animals of a lacertine character.

A cord so pelleted and intertwined with a simple unpelleted
one, gives a very fine effect, and indicates at the same time
more distinctly the existence of two cords in the same interlacement.   This effect is seen more particularly in figure xvi
above, and it occurs again in a remarkable manner on the
fragment of the Oter cross at Braddan, on the fragment of
Ro's cross at the vicarage, Jurby, and on the fragment in the
vestry at Kirk Michael.

Now, if to a single row of pellets running down the centre
of the cord or strap others were subsequently added, and if to

one end of the cord or strap so pelleted a head were added and the other end sharpened off into a tail, we should have at once the serpent or scaly fish, the lizard or dragon, presenting so remarkable an appearance on one or two of the Manx Runic monuments. See figures xx and xxi, associated with figure xxviii.

The Zoomorphic pattern being once established, the inter-twining of monstrous lengthened figures of dogs, birds, fishes, and even men would readily follow. I do not say that such must *necessarily* have been the course of development; but I think it not *improbable*, and certainly it seems worthy of some consideration and more close investigation.

The common twisted rope easily becomes the snake of figure xxviii by the addition of the head and tail, and the pelleted broad strap is easily changed into the lacertine form of figures xx and xxi, but in figures xxii, xxiii, and xxiv, the limbs them-selves of the animal, and more especially the legs and the tail, become the source of knot-work or scroll-ornament.

But the Manx artists were most unhappy in their carving of men and animals. In many instances, such as figures xx, xxi, xxii, xxiii, and xxiv, the evident intention was to produce a *monster;* but, making all allowance for the badness of the material and the effect of weathering, it is too plain that the attempt of the Manx artists to draw animals in their natural form was a miserable failure. Though they were clever enough to design and carve *knot*-work, their *animals* are little better than what a child would draw on a slate. In this respect the Manx cross makers came very far behind their fellow craftsmen in Scotland and Ireland; but this deficiency is to my mind an evidence of the greater antiquity of the Manx crosses. Al-most all the figures of men on Manx crosses are drawn *nude*, the exceptions seeming to belong to a later date.

The great marvel to me in this knot-work ornamentation is the wonderful accuracy with which the artists have managed in all their figures to produce the regular overlap of the cords.

The alternate under and over seems to come without any mistake, however great the number of intertwining cords, and
whatever be the shape of the space which the ornament is
designed to fill. I have traced over many hundred feet of such
knot-work in rubbings from the Manx crosses and have never
found a mistake.

It seems to me as if the artists had made use of actual cords
or ropes in laying down their designs upon these crosses.   Let
anyone take a vacant space, say a square, oblong, or circle, on
a sheet of paper, and endeavour to fill it up with continuous
overlapping cords, and he will perceive the difficulty of working without a design before his eyes.

It is not easy at once to produce such simple results as are
found in figures XIX and XXIX.

Even the various forms of the triquetra found upon the
Manx crosses indicate a considerable amount of ingenuity in
their fabrication and in the manner in which the knot is in-
volved, more especially where it is doubled, tripled, or quad-
rupled, as we see in figure XXIX.

Figures XXXI and XXXII shew the manner in which the heads
of the crosses were filled up, and display much taste.

Certainly, after inspecting the designs on these Runic remains in the Isle of Man, we must give up the idea, if we have
ever entertained it, that the Northmen were altogether a barbarous people, and incapable of any better feelings than those
allied to war and the shedding of blood.

1.—FRAGMENT OF AN INSCRIBED RUNIC CROSS IN BRADDAN CHURCHYARD,
ISLE OF MAN.

INSCRIPTION.—Thurketil raisti crus thano aft Ufaig sun Klinais.

II.

ON SOME MORE RECENTLY DISCOVERED SCANDI-NAVIAN CROSSES IN THE ISLE OF MAN.

BY THE REV. J. G. CUMMING, M.A., F.G.S.

It was remarked in the previous essay on the "Ornamentation of the Runic Monuments in the Isle of Man", that "the preservation of so many crosses in the Isle of Man, belonging to the period in which the island was under the rule of the Northmen, is chiefly owing to the circumstance of their having been subsequently built into the walls of the Parish churches, Peel Cathedral, and Treen chapels". Many of those have been brought to light in the restoration or rebuilding of Manx churches in the present century.

Those discovered prior to 1857 were figured and described in my *Runic and other Monumental Remains of the Isle of Man*, published in that year. The present memoir is supplementary to that work, and is an account of subsequent discoveries up to the present date, and of crosses, the drawings of which were exhibited at the Douglas Meeting of the Cambrian Archæological Association in the year 1865.

I. Woodcut number 1 is the figure of a Runic cross, with inscription, carved on a slab of dark blue schist, three feet six inches in length by one foot ten inches in width, which formed a door-step in the church of Kirk Braddan. It is now placed in the centre of the churchyard, on a mound, along with the two so-called *dragon* crosses. It commemorates Ufeig Klinaison, and was erected by *Thorketil*, or at least by some person whose name began with *Thor*, the terminal runes of the name not being very distinct. In other respects the inscription is very plain and is read Thurketil : Raisti : Crus : Thano : Aft : Ufaig : Sun : Klinais ; and translated " Thorketil erected this cross to Ufeig Klinaison". From the general style of the ornamentation I am disposed to think that this cross may be the workmanship of Gaut Björnson, who appears to have been a noted cross-maker in the Isle of Man in the tenth century.

It exhibits, as a prominent feature in the ornamentation, that beautiful development of knot-work which I have termed *"chain ring-work"*, not occurring, as far as I am aware, on any but Manx crosses, but displayed on the Malbrigd cross at Kirk Michael, which from the inscription we know to have been of Gaut's manufacture. Like the crosses which we know to have been Gaut's, it is also remarkable for the absence of the figures of men and animals so rudely carved on many crosses in the Isle of Man. On the other hand, the inscription might lead us to a different conclusion ; for it is placed at one side of the face of the cross, and not running up the edge, as in the two crosses which bear Gaut's name. Yet it may be noted that in the Malbrigd cross at Kirk Michael, which was carved by Gaut, the latter part of the inscription, for want of more room on the *edge*, is carried into the *face* of the upper portion of the cross. Also in the Thorlaf cross at Ballaugh, which is not improbably of Gaut's workmanship, we have the inscription on one side of the face.

In some alterations and repairs which were made within the last twelve years in the old parish church of Kirk Maughold, the very singular crosses numbered 2, 3, 4, and 5, together with fragments of others, were discovered in the west gable, and as lintels in the chancel.

II. The cross, of which the opposite sides are given in cuts 2 and 3, is a small one taken from the bell-turret of Kirk Maughold Church, to which attention was directed at the visit of the Cambrian Archæological Association in August 1865.

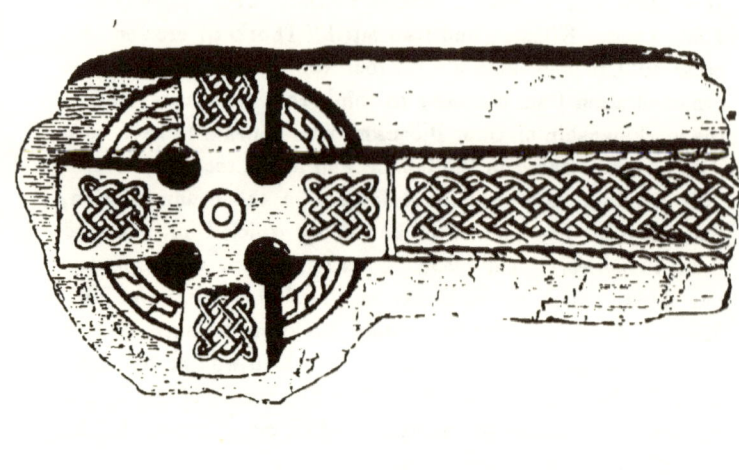

2.   IN KIRK MAUGHOLD CHURCHYARD, ISLE OF MAN.   3.

It contains an intricate development of knot-work on both faces, and that knot-work is contained in panels more after the Irish and Scotch method than is usual in the Manx crosses. An ornamental display of beautiful *chain ring-work* is seen on the fust of the *face* represented in cut 2 ; whilst on the *surface* of the glory about the head of the cross, on the *face* represented in cut 3, we have a species of fret similar to that on the *Oter* cross at Kirk Braddan (the work of Thorburn), on the large Joalf cross at Kirk Michael, probably also his work, and at the left hand corner of the top of the large cross at the entrance to Kirk Maughold churchyard. All these appearances lead me to the presumption that this cross may be of eleventh century date, and somewhat earlier than those numbered 4, 5, 6, in the accompanying cuts. Length, one foot nine inches ; breadth, nine inches. There are traces of an inscription on the edge.

It may be remarked that as yet no inscribed cross, besides the last, has been found in Kirk Maughold parish, and that with the exception of the cross (cuts 2 and 3) which has just been considered, all yet found in that parish differ much from the generality of crosses found elsewhere in the Isle of Man. The Kirk Maughold crosses, as I have before pointed out, approach more than any others to the Scotch type.

It was observed in the previous essay on the "Ornamentation of the Runic Monuments in the Isle of Man", that the church and churchyard of Kirk Maughold, covering three acres, were set apart in ancient times as a Sanctuary.

It is also well known, from Manx history, that there were two Scottish invasions of the Isle of Man under Somerled or Shomhairle Mac Gilbert, Thane of Argyle at the middle of the twelfth century. In the first of these a naval fight occurred in Ramsey Bay on the eve of the Epiphany 1156, with doubtful success, but which led to a compromise between Somerled and Godred Olaveson, king of Man and the Isles. In the second, Somerled, with a fleet of fifty-three ships, came to the Isle of

Man in 1158, defeated Godred, and forced him to flee to the court of Norway to crave assistance. On this second approach of Somerled, the people in the northern part of the Isle of Man conveyed their money and valuables to the Sanctuary of Kirk Maughold, and thither also drove their cattle. According to the *Chronicon Manniæ*, Gil Colum, one of the leaders of the Scotch, planned a nocturnal attack upon this Sanctuary, but was intercepted by a vision of St. Maughold himself, the patron saint of the church, who appeared in Gil Colum's tent, and smote him thrice on the heart with his pastoral staff, so that he expired in great misery and torture.

It is not impossible to connect these crosses with that period, in our endeavour to account for their foreign and Scottish aspect.

III. The cross number 4 is a much worn and partly defaced slab of whinstone, in length four feet six inches, and breadth twenty-two inches. Though Scottish in appearance, the rude manner of treatment of the figures is thoroughly Manx. It is not always easy to determine for what the figures on the Manx crosses were intended. There is, indeed, no mistaking the boar at the sinister side of the base of the fust, as we face it; but we can but conjecture that the figure at the dexter side is intended for a sheep. We have next, above these, on either side, a horse with his rider; one of the horsemen being decked with a helmet or cap, the other bareheaded, as is almost always the case with the human figure on the Manx monuments. The two figures above them, but separated from them on either side by an ornament of knot-work, are undoubtedly monks with their cowls, and seated in antique chairs. We may well compare them with the similar figures on the upper part of the cross at Dunfaldy in Scotland, as given in the *Sculptured Stones of Scotland*, printed for the Spalding Club.

Though the circle or glory about the head of the cross is ornamented with knot-work, it is difficult to make out whether such was the case with the cross itself, though this appears not

4.

CROSS AT KIRK MAUGHOLD, ISLE OF MAN, FORMERLY BUILT INTO THE
WESTERN GABLE OF THE CHURCH.

improbable. A good cast might determine this. The cross is the most prominent part of the slab, and is much roughened by weathering; but it is not easy to decide whether the roughness upon it is due to the weathering alone, or whether it is the remains of some knot-work originally carved thereon, and the outline of which has disappeared. It is, therefore, in the cut left blank.

IV. The appearance of the cross, or rather carved slab, number 5 (in length five feet, and one foot one inch in greatest breadth), is indeed most singular. It is more than usually difficult to determine the objects engraved on it. Probably the figure at the base is meant for a *horse*, whilst the singular figure in the centre, with large eyes and long tapering ears, most corresponds in form with a *hare;* though, as compared with the horse beneath, it is manifestly excessive in size. Yet we may well take into consideration that the human figure above is also too large, as compared with the horse; indeed, it is generally manifest that the Manx artists in their carvings had more regard to the space to be filled up than to the relative magnitude of the objects which they intended to represent.

This animal appears to be caught upon the head by a lasso, or some such instrument, as it is in the act of issuing from a hole in a rock after the manner of the mountain hares in the Isle of Man.

As to the man represented at the head of the slab, we can only make out that he appears to be bearing a shield in his left *hand* rather than upon the left *arm*, and that his right hand grasps something which we may conjecture to be a sword. The shield has upon it a reversed figure of Z, which is the Manx later Runic symbol for " S", and may be put as the initial letter of the word " skiöllar", a shield. If it be simply an ornament it may be compared with the ornamentation on the upper part of one of the edges of the large cross at the entrance to Kirk Maughold churchyard ; this large cross bearing on the face of it also two naked human figures.

c

v. The sixth woodcut represents a cross which is to be seen in a Treen chapel in Kirk Maughold parish, not far from Ballaglass Waterfall. In length it is five feet, in width eighteen inches. I exhibited a rubbing from it at the Douglas Meeting of the Cambrian Archæological Association; and during the excursion of the Society to the north of the Isle of Man, Mr. Blight made the accompanying admirable sketch of it. The nude human figure on the lower portion, or fust of the cross, allies it with the Kirk Maughold and Scottish types; whilst the knot-work in the head of the cross differs considerably in arrangement from that on any other of the Manx crosses, the work being of a more open character, and presenting an absence of continuity in the knot-work. The nearest approach to it is the Niel Lumgun cross at Kirk Michael, which I have pointed out as of a more foreign character and later date than the generality of the inscribed crosses. The human figure on this cross is not unlike that at the upper part of the eastern edge of the Joalf cross at Kirk Michael, though the latter bears a shield. The long pointed beard assimilates it with the figures on the remarkable slab found in the old chapel of the Calf of Man, and now in possession of the Clerk of the Rolls at Castletown. It appears to be truly Scandinavian, and of the twelfth century.

As this present memoir was called forth by the visit of the Cambrian Archæological Association to the Isle of Man, it is an evidence of the value of the Society's labours in directing the attention of local antiquaries to the deeper study of the antiquarian remains in the places which are from time to time visited.

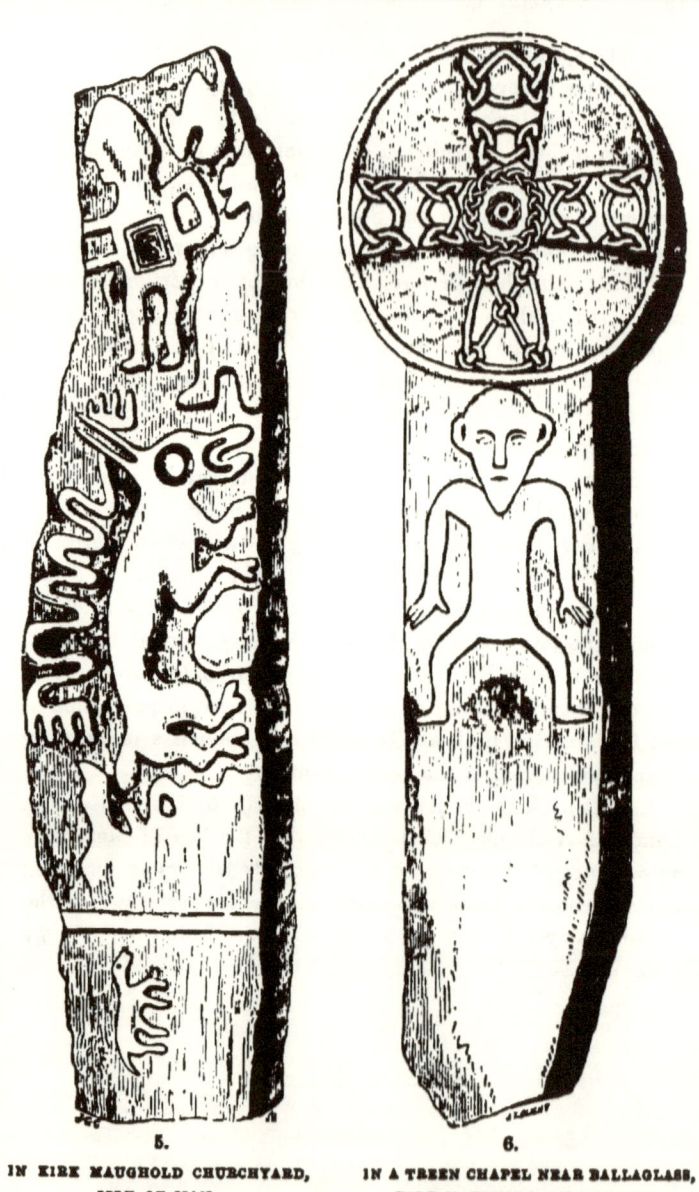

5.

IN KIRK MAUGHOLD CHURCHYARD,
ISLE OF MAN.

6.

IN A TREEN CHAPEL NEAR BALLAGLASS,
KIRK MAUGHOLD, ISLE OF MAN.

III.

THE RUNIC INSCRIPTIONS OF THE
ISLE OF MAN.

BY THE REV. J. G. CUMMING, M.A., F.G.S.

NOWHERE in so small a space are there so many monumental inscriptions in Runic characters and in the Norse language as in the Isle of Man.

Within an area of not more than twenty miles in length by twelve in width, no less than eighteen of such inscriptions have been discovered, and it is probable that there are many more undiscovered, and there have certainly been many destroyed or lost.

If the Norse language were not at one time prevalent in the island, it must at any rate have been well understood, so as to be used in monumental inscriptions in preference to the Celtic or the Latin.

The marvel now seems to be that, excepting the names of places, we meet with so few, if any, traces of the Norse language in the modern Manx. In the English language we know there are several traces of the ancient Danish occupation of our country, though the Northmen were not in power in England for anything like the time during which they ruled in the Isle of Man. The Celtic is not cognate to the Norse, whereas the Anglo-Saxon is. Hence the Norse soon died out in the Isle of Man on the expulsion of the Northmen, not being readily moulded into Manx ; just as the Manx itself is now dying out before the English.   .

c 2

Having been engaged for some time in decyphering the inscriptions on the Manx Runic monuments, not always an easy
task, through the wear and tear of time, and in many cases
their fragmentary condition, I venture to offer for consideration
the readings and interpretations which I have concluded to be
the most probable, subject of course to such corrections as a
still closer examination and more accurate judgment may determine to be necessary.

I may say that I think the most secure method of coming at
the readings is that which I have myself in most cases adopted,
viz., by making plaster of Paris casts of these inscriptions and
then taking rubbings on the raised edges of the moulds, for the
inscriptions are all incised. The rubbings thus made upon the
moulds come out clearer than those made on the original stones.
The material of the casts also being white, and the objects
readily turned about so as to catch the light, the shadows thus
originated will sometimes enable us to decypher the inscriptions with greater ease than we can upon the dark clay schist
of which the inscribed crosses are made, and which are mostly
fixed in one position.

After much consideration, I have not seen reason to alter in
any very material degree the *readings* I obtained ten years
ago, and gave in my *Runic and other Monumental Remains of
the Isle of Man*, published in 1857, but the *interpretations* are
here amended. The emendations which I am now enabled to
give upon my previous interpretations are due for the most
part to the valued suggestions of Ralph Carr, Esq., S.A.S.C.,
of Hedgeley, near Alnwick, than whom no one has shown himself more skilled in the interpretation of Scandinavian and
Anglo-Saxon inscriptions, and to whom I would express the
highest obligations. Since I resided on the island other monuments have been discovered, two of them, at least, inscribed
with runes; and happily these are very nearly perfect inscriptions, and may be read with slight hesitation, even on the
photographs of the crosses. I refer to the two placed in the

centre of Braddan churchyard, near the well-known so-called
Dragon cross, within the last twelve years.

One thing which greatly facilitates the reading of the inscriptions is their general uniformity of expression, the words "raisti
crus thana" *(erected this cross)* or " raist runer" *(carved the
runes)* being of constant occurrence. The difficulty is rather
in the *names* where some of the letters are imperfect or very
faintly traced.

Many of the Runic letters consist of one straight vertical
stroke, the alteration in the power of them depending on the
arrangement of one or two lines meeting them slantwise on
either side. Unfortunately the nature of the stone (clay schist),
of which all the *incised* Manx crosses are made, is such that,
on weathering, lines or cracks are apt to present themselves
crossing the vertical lines of the runes, and creating the appearance of incisions where none at first were made.

The similarity also of the runes for R and U, when badly
formed, not unfrequently presents a difficulty in the reading, more especially if the rune has undergone a slight deface-
ment.

We have also to make allowance both for imperfect spelling
and varieties of dialect in the inscriptions. Thus the common
word "thana" *(this)* is written thana, thano, thona, thono, thanu,
thua, thenr, and thensi, the variety in some cases, no doubt,
caused by inflection. The word "aftir *(to)* is written also aiftir,
aft, af, eft, and eftir. Again, the word "raisti" *(erected)*, not
to be confounded with "raist" *(carved)*, is written also risti,
and raiti.

Gaut himself, who seems to have been a noted cross manu-
facturer in the Isle of Man, on two of the crosses bearing his
name, writes *thana* and *thano, gurthi* and *girthi.*

There is one thing which is particularly worth noticing in
these inscriptions, and that is the entire absence of any request
for a prayer on behalf of the departed. On the Irish crosses
we constantly meet with. the request "Or do," and on the

.

Anglo-Saxon we find the words "Gibiddad dher saule," *pray for the soul*, or "Gicegæd heosum sawlum," *pray for their souls*, but we have nothing of the kind on the Manx crosses. Perhaps we may, from this circumstance, infer the original character of the Manx crosses, and that the Northmen in the Isles did not owe their Christianity to the same source as the Irish and Anglo-Saxons. Further, the absence of any such request on the Manx crosses makes considerably against those who would have us believe that the Manx cross makers were mere copyists from Irish models, and supports the views, which I have elsewhere expressed, as to the ornamentation of the Manx monuments, viz., that it is completely *sui generis*, and not borrowed from another people.

To proceed with the inscriptions, as given in the plate :—

1. On a very beautiful cross, which stands on the south side of the churchyard gate of Kirk Michael, we have the following inscription (see plate fig. 1). MAIL : BRIGDI : SUNR : ATHAKANS : SMITH : RAISTI : CRUS : THANO : FUR : SALU : SINI : SIN : BRUKUIN : GAUT : GIRTHI : THANO : AUGALA : I MAUN. This inscription is *incised*, as all the inscriptions are on the Manx monuments. The portion running upwards from the base and ending with the word "Gaut" is carved along the *edge* of the stone on the right hand as you look at the principal face; then, on the *front* of the cross, on the same side above the glory, occur the words "Girthi thano auk"; then, above the glory, on the opposite side of the same face, we read the remaining words, ala : I Maun. There can hardly be a mistake about the runes, as they were deeply carved, and remain very distinct, but, owing to an apparent violation of the laws of Norse grammar, the interpretation of the inscription is not so certain.

The learned Scandinavian interpreters, Professors Münch and Worsäae, have translated it thus :—

"Malbrigd, son of Athakan (the) Smith, erected this cross for his Soul. . . . Gaut made this and all in Man."

The words "Sin brukuin" are left untranslated.

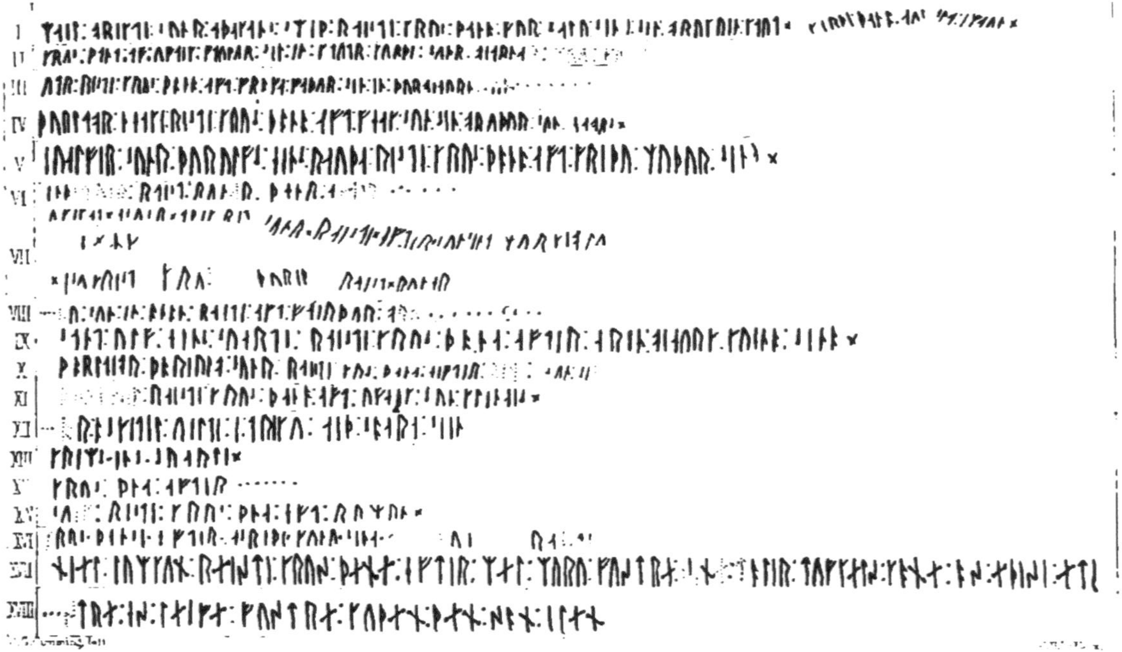

I

II

III

IV

V

VI

VII

VIII

IX

X

XI

XII

XIII

XIV

XV

XVI

XVII

XJL T.- Runes are incised. In ... (this) picture in later Manx Runes. The dotted letters in the other picture are heights.

I ventured to give in my *Runic and other Monumental Remains of the Isle of Man* the translation thus:—"Malbrigd, the son of Athakan the Smith, erected this cross for his soul, (but) his kinsman Gaut made it and all in Man."

Mr. Carr objects very strongly and properly to Smith and Gaut being considered as in any other case than the accusative. The nominatives would be Smithr and Gautr, and the genitive of Smithr would be Smithar.

My own impression is that these Norse stone cutters might make mistakes in grammar as well as in spelling, which we know they have done, as above stated. In doing this they seem sometimes to have been guided by the space they had at command on the stone, and it has occurred to me that the false grammar in the above inscription may be due to a like cause. Perhaps on account of want of space at the end of the incision, the two words, "I Maun" were written as one without any stop between them, whilst at the beginning of it, where the space had not been calculated, the name Mailbrigdi is divided by a stop into the words, as Mail : Brigdi.

But Mr. Carr's reasonings on the score of grammar are so just and forcible, that I must give them in full. He says—"We must ever remember that unless we can make out the exact grammatical construction of an old Norse or of an Anglo-Saxon inscription, we must leave it in obscurity. The cases of the nouns, adjectives, and pronouns, and the tenses and persons of the verbs, are the only means we have of convincing ourselves and others that we are right; the old Norse is nearly as rich as the Latin in its cases, and which are most wonderfully observed. Writers could no more confound or omit them than a Frenchman could use the wrong genders of a noun or the wrong tense of a verb in speaking. The right ones come to him with his mother's milk, and he cannot mistake them. Hence the accuracy of Icelandic or old Norse inscriptions, and of Saxon ones, and of old Roman ones in Latin, as to cases, genders, tenses, etc. And these very things are the proofs to us that we are reading aright. The moment we find wrong grammar we are at sea, and merely guessing, however plausible the same may seem to us. And grammar makes all compromise impossible, unless where both readings happen to be equally grammatical, and you choose the most likely all things considered. Thus, I have no quarrel with Smith, if we can make grammar of it; but it must stand for Smithar or nothing, if from the noun supposed."

Mr. Carr hence, in the first place, suggested that the word SMITH *might* be written for SMEITI or SMEIT, since " ei" in runes is often written simple "i". Now, the word SMEITR means *contusion* or figuratively *contrition*, and in the dative or ablative it would be SMEIT, signifying *in a contusion* or perhaps *in contrition*, and the inscription might then be translated—" Maelbrigd, son of Athakan, in hurt (or contrition) raised this cross for his soul. His betrothed caused Gaut to chisel it in Man."

Mr. Carr has secondly suggested that, instead of regarding " Smith" as part of the personal pronoun Smithr, a workman, we may take it directly as the feminine noun " Smidh", a fabric or work of art, and in the accusative case, thus making the whole inscription grammatical.

Again, as GAUT must be in the accusative, we must have a verb to govern it, and this we have in the word OIRTHI, which follows it, and signifies to *cause* or *make* to do a thing, as well as to *fashion, form,* or *make.* It is in fact often used like our English word *make*, as an auxiliary verb. Mr. Carr further observes that, as there is no stop between the words AUK and ALA, but only a break caused by the transfer of the inscription to the other side of the stone, it may well be read as one word AUGALA, and as AU and o nearly sound the same, the word may be for OGALA, " to chisel with a mallet."

With respect to the word BRUKUIN, it may well be rendered *bride* or *betrothed.* Hence the whole inscription would stand thus :—

MAIL-BRIGDI, SUNR ATHAKANS, SMIDH RAISTI CRUS THANO FUR
SALU SINI :

SIN BRUKUIN GAUT GIRTHI THANO AUGALA I MAUN.

And may be translated thus :—

"Mailbrigd, son of Athakan, as a work of art, erected this
cross for his soul. His betrothed (or bride) made (or caused)
Gaut to chisel it in Man."

The expression raised this cross may merely mean *made provision for it*, whilst the direction of the work during his decline from wounds or sickness was undertaken by his Manx
bride, the natural executrix, and the expression *in Man* would
imply that the inscription might afterwards be read by new
comers from Norway or Denmark, who might otherwise think
the stone had been cut elsewhere, Mailbrigd himself having
been not improbably a new comer.

Mailbrigd (the servant of Bridget) is evidently of Celtic origin, and a name not unfrequent in the annals of these countries. One of the churches in the Isle of Man is dedicated in
honour of St. Bridget, as well as the nunnery near Douglas.

My own idea still is that the AR in SMITHAR has been dropped
on account of the next word RAISTI beginning with R, and the
two words SMITHARRAISTI read together would not sound very
different from SMITHRAISTI. Hence I shall prefer retaining
SMITH as an appellative, considering it as in the genitive in
apposition with the name ATHAKANS, and give, as the result
the following translation :—"Malbrigd, the son of Athakan,
the smith, raised (or caused to be raised) this cross for his
soul. His betrothed caused Gaut to chisel it in Man."

In any case, the great advantage of reading AUGALA *to chisel
with a mallet*, instead of AUK ALA *and all*, will be apparent.
First it gets rid of the false grammar of regarding the word
GAUT as a nominative, and then sets aside the presumption that
Gaut was the earliest cross maker, and the only one in Man of
his day. This suggestion is entirely due to Mr. Carr.

It is well to note that the name of the Isle of Man on this

cross is spelt MAUN, showing that it was anciently pronounced broad, and thus bringing it into closer connection with the name Mona, the Roman appellation of the island.

II. I will take next the inscription on a very much worn and defaced cross, which stands on a green near the churchyard gate of Kirk Andreas, and which also is the work of Gaut.

The first and last portions of the inscription are too much injured to be read with any certainty, but we may make out distinctly.

CRUS : THANA : AF : UFAIG : FAUTHUR : SIN : IN : GAUTR : GIRTHI : SUNR : BIARNAH. (See fig. II). The word before " Crus" was almost certainly *Raisti*, but the name has disappeared. The translation would be

" (NN erected) this cross to Ufeig, his father, but Gaut Björnson made it."

After " Sunr Bjarnar" (Björnson, the son of the bear) occur some runes which look like *Cub Culi*.

Mr. Carr has pointed out that "kobbi" signifies a *seal* or *sea-calf*, and that "culi" may stand for "queli", *i.e., killer*. Hence if the reading be " cub culi," *seal killer*, it may be an agnomen of Gaut, indicating that he had previously been in his youth a noted *seal hunter*, though after his residence in Man becoming a stone cutter.

I take next the inscriptions on three crosses, all of which I believe to have been the work of one and the same artist, Thorburn, a name still permanent in the Isle of Man.

My reasons for coming to the conclusion that they are all the work of this artist are that on all three of them occurs the same remarkable lacertine ornament, and on all are the words *risti* for *raisti*, *aft* for *aftir*, and *thono* for *thana*.

III. The first of the three is that on the fragment of the *Oter* cross in the midst of Kirk Braddan churchyard. It reads (see fig. III)—UTR : RISTI : CRUS : THONO : AFT : FROKA : FATHUR : SIN : IN : THURDIAURN : SUNR.

" Oter (or Otter) erected this cross to his Father Frogat, but Thorbjörn (or Thorburn) son of (NN made it)."

The name of Thorburn's father and the word *girthi* "made it" are broken off, but no doubt these were the words originally there.

There was an Oter (Otter or Octar) appointed Viceroy of Man by Magnus Barbeen in 1098, and this date agrees with the period (the tenth and eleventh centuries) assigned to the majority of the Manx crosses by Professors Münch and Worsäae. Gaut was probably the maker of most of the earlier crosses in the tenth century, and Thorburn, whose crosses are more elaborately finished and dialect somewhat different, may have been an artist of the latter part of the eleventh or the beginning of the twelfth century.

IV. Alongside of the *Oter* cross is another of like design but more perfect, viz., the *Thorlaf* (or Dragon) cross, the inscription on which is very perfect and legible. It runs thus (see fig. IV) — THURLABR : NEAKI : RISTI : CRUS : THONO : AFT : FEAK : SUN : SIN : BRUTHUR : SUN : EABRS.

"Thorlaf Neake erected this cross to Feake his son, Brother's son of Jaf."

V. The third of Thorburn's crosses is the magnificent Joalf cross at the churchyard gate of Kirk Michael, the inscription on which is very plain, and reads (see fig. V)—JUALFR : SUNR : THURULFS : EINS : RAUTHA : RISTI : CRUS : THONO : AFT : FRITHU : MUTHUR : SINA :

"Joalf the son of Thorjolf the Red erected this cross to his Mother Frida."

VI. Having taken now the inscriptions on five of the crosses, of which we believe the makers to have been Gaut and Thorburn, we will take an inscription which contains also the name of the maker of the cross, but no other name.

It is on a fragment of the lower portion of a cross which stands in a corner on the south side of the church of St. John the Baptist near the Tynwald-hill. The inscription is very much worn and defective both at the beginning and end (see fig. VI). The four first runes are tolerably plain, but the next four are very imperfect, and the great similarity of the runes for *R* and *U*, as I have before observed, throws some doubt over the reading. Mr. Kneale has proposed *Ino : Sunr*, "Ino's son." This will require us to read the fourth rune, as two dots or a cross for the separation of the word instead of *S*, but a very close and repeated inspection of casts leads me still to read the fourth rune as *S*, and then after the *S* there are certainly more runes than *UNR*. That the last rune is *R*, I have little doubt, and that the letter after *S* may be *U* is not improbable, but there are still two letters remaining, of which the first may be R or U, and the other I, E, A, B, O, or N. The inscription will then read INOSRUIR : RAIST : RUNAR : THESR : AFTIR ; *i. e.*, "Inosruir carved these runes to (NN)."

VII. We have still another Manx cross-maker's name, but upon a work of which he has no need to be proud, for it is a mere slab of clay schist, with a very rude figure of a cross and glory upon it, and the runes are scrawled over it, up, down, and crosswise on both sides of the slab with little apparent connection between them.

On one face of the slab at the top and running upwards we have the word "Cru," part of the word CRUS, *cross*. Underneath it, running downwards, ISUCRIST, *Jesus Christ*, placed where the body of our Lord would be on the cross, and near the bottom, running slantwise, THURITH, *Thurith*, then, on the edge at the bottom, RAIST × RUNER, *carved the runes*.

On the other face of the slab we have a number of words placed up and down (βουστροφηδον), the connection of which it is difficult to make out. On the right hand side of the face, as we look at it, running downwards and very faintly traced, are simply the runes AM × I, the fragments of two words; running upwards there are UGIGAT (or AGEGAT) × ASUIR × ATHIGRIT, on the opposite edge, running upwards, we read SUNR × RAISTI × AFTIR × SUN × SIS A (see fig. VII), and then running downwards the word MURKIBLU.

The letters are all badly formed and much worn, being on

the face of the stone, which was exposed and knocked about for some time on a piece of rock-work in a garden at Kirk Conchan. The strokes in the runes, which should be vertical, slope considerably, and the side strokes are often too much prolonged. Hence we can readily read the word "Ugigat" as "Agegat," which, as Mr. Carr has well remarked, will enable us to give some meaning to this otherwise obscure inscription. For "Agegat" may be an abbreviated form of "Agegnat," which means *over against*, then "Asuir" may be for "Osuir," *our*. The grammar requires that we should read "Aftir Sun *Sin*, not "*Sina*," and this we may properly do, for the "a" is in fact separated from the "Sin" by a line forming a portion of the rude figure of a cross scratched on the face of the stone, and this line may be considered as equivalent to the usual mark separating words. We can then further regard this "a" as a preposition governing the word "Murkiblu," though it is on the other side of the slab, and "Murkiblu" may be read as "Murkibla," signifying *mirk-blue* or *dark-blue*, *i.e.*, *mourning*.

Further, we may observe that a portion of the slab (doubtless containing some words before "Agegat") is broken off. Hence the inscription may be put together thus :—

"...AM ✕ I ... AGEGAT ✕ ASUIR ✕ ATHIGRIT ✕ ... SUNR ✕ RAISTI ✕ AFTIR ✕ SUN ✕ SIN ✕ A ✕ MURKIBLA, and we can then translate it.

".... am I .... (lies buried) over against our Athigrit, (NN's) son erected (this) to his son, in mourning."

The inscription, though imperfect, is thus rendered intelligible, and is one full of affection and sad remembrance.

VIII. I am not aware of the names of any other makers occurring on the Manx crosses, but probably there was the name of one upon the cross, a fragment of which is in the garden of the vicarage at Jurby. I am not without hope that the remainder of the cross may still be discovered. The portion of the inscription remaining (written βουστροφηδον) reads thus (see fig. VIII).

"... RU : SUN : IN : ONON : RAITI : AFT : FAITHUR : BRU.
"... Ro's Son, but Onon erected it to his Father's Brother."
Ru may be merely the termination of a name or the name
itself. In either case it seems to be connected with the maker
of the cross, whoever he may have been. "Sun" must be in
the accusative case. The "Raiti" seems misspelt for "raisti,"
raised; if we could read it "raist," carved, then we should
have Onon as another cross maker. The "Bru" is either part
of the word Bruthur, or of the name of the father of Onon.

I will pass more rapidly over the remaining inscriptions,
which, with one exception, are of a less interesting character.

IX. On the cross which I have called the *Sandulf* cross in
Andreas churchyard is the following inscription (see fig. IX).

SAND : ULF : EINS : SUARTI : RAISTI : CRUS : THONA : AFTIR : ARIN :
BIAURK : KUINO : SINO.

"Sandulf the Swarthy erected this cross to his wife Arinbjörg."

The most remarkable part of this inscription is the division
of the names Sandulf and Arinbjörg each into two words, just
as Mail Brigdi is separated in inscription I. On the cross is
the figure of a female, perhaps Arinbjörg, on horseback.

X. On a very beautiful and almost perfect cross which stands
in the churchyard of the old parish church of Ballaugh, is the
following inscription, which runs up one side of the face of the
fust of the cross, and into the cavity between the arms (see
fig. X).

THORLAIBR : THORIULB : SUNR : RAISTI : CRS : THONA : AIFTIR : ULB :
SUN : SIN.

"Thorlaf, the son of Thorjölf, erected this cross to Olave
his son."

In order apparently to save space, the carver has omitted
the rune for *U* in Crus, crowded the runes *Ulb* (Olave) and put
Sun Sin in the head of the cross. And yet he writes *Aiftir*
for *Aftir*.

XI. On a cross which had formed the doorstep of Braddan

church, but which is now placed in the midst of the churchyard, we have the following very nearly perfect inscription
(see fig. XI) :—

THURKETIL : RAISTI : CRUS : THANO : AFT ; UFAIG : SUN : KLINAIS.

" Thorketil erected this cross to Ufeig Klinaison."

There is some doubt about the first name, though the first
syllable seems very like *Thur*, and the next five upright marks
appear to me to stand best as the runes for *ketil*. Mr. Kneale
has remarked on the number of Norse names beginning with
Thor, as Thörbjörn, Thorfinnr, Thorketil, Thorstein, Thorvaldr,
to which we may add from the above inscriptions Thorlaibr and
Thoriulb. To my eye the runes in this inscription altogether
look most like Thurketil, and I adopt this name. The termination *ketil* is very frequent in Norse, and has been corrupted
in English into *kettle*. Thus there are in a parish in Suffolk
with which I am acquainted the names *Tirkettle* (Thorketil),
Ashkettle (Osketil), and *Rinkettle* (Runketil). The two first
Norse names occur on Manx crosses, and in the same Suffolk
parish there is also the Norse name *Feake*, the Feak of the
Braddan cross.

XII. On the fragment of a cross originally at Kirk Michael,
but now in the Museum at Distington, we have the singular
inscription (see fig. XII)

ER : OSKETIL : VILDI : I : DRIKU : AITH : SOARA : SIIN.

The Scandinavian *savans* read this ASKITIL : VILTI : I : TRIGU :
AITHSOARA : SIIN, translating it—

" Whom Askitil deceived in security, contrary to his pledge
of peace."

A close examination of the cast of this stone enabled me to
detect an ER at the beginning, and the stop between "Aith"
and " Soara," which I pointed out to Mr. Carr, and the result
of the amended reading has led to some valuable hints as to
the translation, and given a totally different character to the
inscription.

I would first observe, as I have done in the table of Alphabets appended to my *Runic and other Monumental Remains*, that the Manx alphabet contains no rune for *h*. The first word, therefore, in this inscription " Er" is put for " Her," *here*.

Next, the third word, " vildi," is derived from "vila," to *bewail*, and is not to be read for "villdi," from "villa"," to *beguile, deceive* or *seduce*.

The fifth word must be read " driku", *drink*, and " i driku" will mean *in a drinking*, i. e., *in a funereal feast*, which we know was always accompanied with ale drinking amongst the Norse and Saxons.

The next word, " Aith," is most probably a female proper name.

Then "Soara" is an old form of spelling for "Svara," a *mother-in-law*, the Latin *socrus*.

Siin is another method of representing the long sound of the I in SIN.

Putting all these readings together we get the inscription as, ER : OSKETIL : VILDI : I : DRIKU : AITH : SOARA : SIIN.

" Here Osketel bewailed in a drinking feast Aitha his mother-in-law."

XIII. We have at Kirk Michael fragments of three crosses bearing inscriptions (see figures XIII, XIV, and XV).

The first is in the vestry of Kirk Michael Church, GRIMS : INS : SAURTI. " Grims the Black."

XIV. The next, which is in the churchyard wall, is SVIG : RISTI : CRUS : TIINA : EFT : RUMUN. " Svig erected this cross to Romon."

The Svig is not very plain. On another fragment of the same cross we have simply the letters NT.

XV. The third inscription also on the churchyard wall is CRUS : TIINA : AFTIR. " This cross to   ."

XVI. In the walls of the nave of Peel Cathedral is built the fragment of a cross bearing this inscription (see fig. XVI)— . . . US : THENSI : EFTIR : ABRITHI : KUNU : SINA : DUTUR : UT . . . RAIST.

Filling up the inscription as far as we can, it may be translated " (AB erected) this cross to his wife Asrith, the daughter of Oter; (CD) carved (the runes)."

The first three runes in *Dutur* are imperfect, and the word may be *Mutur*, "Mother."

The name Oter has before been noticed on the Braddan cross. If the stone were extracted from the wall of the Cathedral we might perhaps be able to form a conjecture from the style of ornamentation as to whether the two Oters were the same person.

XVII. The word *Kunu* for *Kuinu* "Wife", seems to point to a later dialect, which we have in the next inscription which is on that cross on the churchyard wall of Kirk Michael, which has been before noticed as having a more foreign aspect than the other Manx crosses, and the runes upon which are spoken of by Professor Münch as being of a later date, differing from the older Manx runes in the letters A, D, N, and S.

NIAL : LUMGUN : RAISTI : CRUS : THANA : EFTIR : MAL : MURU : FUSTRA : SINA : DOTIR : DUFGALS : KONA : OS : ATHISI : ATI.

In my *Runic and other Monumental Remains, etc.*, I translated *Kona* "Keen," following Professor Münch, though differing from him in the reading and translation in other respects. I have more lately been informed by my friend David Forbes, Esq., F.R.S., a Manxman and brother to the late much lamented Professor Ed. Forbes, that in the wild and more primitive interior of Norway the word *Kona* is still used for *Wife*, to which the *Kunu* of the previously named inscription approximates. Further than this, *Kona* is not the genitive, as it ought to be if rendered *Keen*, and agreeing with *Dufgals*.

It is also questionable if such a word as " os" occurs in the accusative for *whom*; but, remembering that the Manx had no rune for *h*, it may well be put for " hos," *i.e.*, " hues," in the genitive signifying *of whom* or *whose*.

The translation of the inscription will then be—

"Niel Lumgun erected this cross to Maelmore, his foster

D

child, the daughter of Dugald, whose wife (widow) Athisi he possessed."

This makes very plain sense. Niel Lumgun married Athisi, the widow of Dugald; hence Maelmore, the daughter of Dugald by Athisi, would become the *step-daughter* or *foster child* of Lumgun. Mr. Carr, objecting to Athisi as a proper name of a woman, conceives that it may be put for the word ATVISTI, which is dative and ablative, from ATVIST, "existence" or "being", and would render the latter part of the inscription "whose wife (or widow) in lifetime he had".

In an extract, apparently from the Niala Saga, contained in the *Antiquitates Scandicæ*, we learn that in the year 996 the Nialsons Grim and Helgi, together with one Kari, slew in Man Dungal, son of the King of Man, and that in 1014 one Gunnr Lambasonr was slain by Kari in Rossey. The Niel Lumgun of the above inscription looks so like Gunnr Lambasonr that we might possibly connect him or his kin with it. The inscription joins a Niel Lumgun with a Dugald, and Kari slew both a Dugald and a Gunnr Lambasonr. If this Dugald were the son of the King of Man in 996, he was son of Godred III and brother of Reginald II, of the line of Orry. But all the names are so common in Manx history of that date that it is quite unsafe to connect these monuments with any particular persons. There was a Helgi, King of Man in 894; and according to the Egilla Saga one Nial or Neil was king in 914, and we have before (inscription XIII) met with the name Grim, but we have no right to connect the Grim of that inscription with the Grim the son of Nial and brother of Helgi of the Niala Saga.

In connection with the supposition that the Dugald of our inscription might be the son of Goddred III and an elder brother of Reginald II, it may be well to note that, as before observed, the Manx having no rune for H, the ATI of the inscription may be put for HATI, signifying "called" or "named", and the KONA may be translated in the higher sense of "Queen". Hence KONA OS ATHISI ATI might even be rendered "Queen by us in lifetime called". We can well imagine Maelmore, the granddaughter of Godred III, to be called "Queen" on the death of her father Dugald. Perhaps she died soon after her father. Her step-father, Niel Lumgun, who erected the cross, would certainly be the enemy of Kari who slew Dugald, and so afterwards engaging with him in Ross, was himself killed by the hand of the slayer of his step-daughter's own father. This cross may therefore have been erected to a Queen of Man, whose name was Maelmore.

XVIII. The only remaining Manx Runic inscription, as far as at present known, is that which is given in Camden's *Britannia*, Gibson's édition, p. 1458, and which is from a stone said to have been built into the wall of the old church of Kirk Michael. It is in the same later Manx Runes as the last noticed inscription. Casts of it are in the possession of Sir Henry Dryden, Bart., of Canons Ashby, and in the Museum of the Archæological Institute, which were taken by Mr. Balley. The stone cannot now be found. The inscription, which runs thus, is imperfect :—

STRA : ES : LAIFA : FUSTRA : GUTHAN : THAN : SON : ILAN. (See fig. XVIII.)

The "Stra" must be part of "Fostra," and in the accusative case. The "Guthan" will be the same as "Godhan" or "Goodhan," *good*, whilst the "Ilan" may be put for "Illan," *ill* or *evil*.

Mr. Carr thinks that the ES LEIFA may be read as a compound word ISLEIFA, the accusative of ISLEIFI, *ice-giant;* and that the word Eft may have come before the first Fostra; and that " A," *towards*, is understood before Than. He proposes, therefore, to read the inscription (EFT : FO) : STRA : ISLEIFA : FOSTRA : GUDHAN : (A) : THAN : SON : ILAN, and translate it—

"To foster father Isleif, the good foster father, towards an evil son."

I can conjecture no better rendering for this obscure and fragmentary inscription.

child, the daughter of Dug...

This makes very plain sense. Nic...

the widow of Dugald; hence Maelmo... the step-...

Dugald by Athisl, would become the ...objecting to Athisl...

child of Lamgan. Mr. Carr, objecting to Athisl... may be put for... "exi...

...conceives that it may be put for... ATVIST, "exi...

ATVIST, which is dative and ablative, from ATVIST, part of the inscrip...

or "being", and would render the latter part of the inscription...

"whose wife (or widow) in lifetime he had".

In an extract, apparently from the Niala Saga, contained ;

the Antiquitates Scandicæ, we learn that in the year 996 th...

Niolmor Grim and Helgi, together with one Kari, slew in M...

Dungal, son of the King of Man, and that in 1014 one Gun...

Lambasonr was slain by Kari in Rossey. The Niol Lumg...

of the above inscription looks so like Gunnr Lambasonr that...

might possibly connect him or his kin with it. The inscrip...

joins a Niol Lamgan with a Gunnr Lambasonr. If this Dugald and be...

Dugald and a Gunnr Lambasonr. If this Dugald and Kari slew th...

of Reginald II, of the line of Orry. But all the names...

the King of Man in 996, he was son of Godred III and...

...in Manx history of that date that it is quite un...

...connect these movements with any particular persons.

...a Helgi, King of Man in 894; and according...

before (inscription xiii) met with the name Grim, but...

the son of Nial or Neil was king in 914, and...

Reila Saga one Nial or Neil was king in 914, but...

In connexion with the Grim of that inscription with...

inscription might be the son of Helgi of the Niala Sa...

brother of Reginald II, the supposition that the Du...

observed, the Manx having no rune for s, the ATI a...

tion may be put for KARI, signifying "called" or...

the STISL or ATIVSI ATI may be translated in the higher sens...

Hence STISL or ATIVSI ATI might even be rende...

IV.

RUSHEN ABBEY IN THE ISLE OF MAN.

BY THE REV. J. G. CUMMING, M.A., F.G.S.

THE ruins of Rushen Abbey, or of the Abbey of St. Mary of Russin, are situated on the western bank of the Silverburn, close by the village of Ballasalla, in the parish of Malew, and Sheading of Rushen, two miles north of Castletown, Isle of Man.

This abbey was an offshoot of the Abbey of St. Mary of Furness, which received a grant of lands in the Isle of Man from Olavo Godredson, King of Man and the Isles, in or about the year 1134. The original charter of Olavo, granting these lands to Furness Abbey, does not appear, but reference is made to it in another charter of the same king, and of that same year (1134), which is preserved amongst the *Chartæ Miscellaneæ* in the office of the Duchy of Lancaster (vol. i, fol. 30; see also vol. vii, Manx Society, p. 1), granting for ever to the Abbey of St. Mary of Furness the election of the Bishop of Sodor and Man. These grants were subsequently confirmed by Godred and Reginald, Kings of Man in 1154 and 1188, and by a bull of Eugenius III to Furness Abbey in 1152, and further by bulls of Urban III in 1186, and Celestine III in 1194.

It is also stated in the *Chronicon Manniæ et Insularum* (written by the monks of Rushen Abbey), under date 1134, that "Olavus Rex dedit Yvoni Abbati de Furness, partem terre sue in Mannia ad abbatiam constituendam in loco qui vocatur Russin". It appears, however, from the chartulary of Furness,

that this grant of lands had in the first instance been offered
to the Abbey of Rievalle or Rivaulx,—" Certa terra in Mannia
data fuit Abbatie de Rievalle ad construendam Abbatiam de
Russin, postea tamen data fuit Abbatie Furnesie ad construendam eam de ordine Cisterciensi ubi modo scituata est et sic
non de Rievalle sed de Furnesio exivit."

In the aforesaid bull of Eugenius III mention is also made
of a monastery of St. Leoc in the Isle of Man,—" In Mannia
ex dono nobilis viri Olavi, Regis Insularum, terras de Carnec-
let usque ad Monasteriam Sancti Leoc cum appendiciis suis";
from which we must conclude either that the Abbey of Rushen
was originally known by the name of St. Leoc, or that another
monastery had previously existed in the Isle of Man, which
became absorbed in that of St. Mary of Rushen. Some countenance is given to this latter supposition by the statement of
Sacheverell in his *Short Survey of the Isle of Man* (p. 34, vol. i,
Manx Society), that " one Mac Marus, a person of great
prudence, moderation, and justice, in the year 1098 laid the
first foundation of the Abbey of Rushen in the town of Balla-
salley"; and he goes on further to say (p. 36) that " Olave,
the third son of Goddard Crovan, anno 1134, gave the Abbey
of Rushen, some years before begun by Mac Marus, to Evan
(Ivo), Abbot of Furness, which was to. serve as a nursery to
the church." Unfortunately, Sacheverell has not referred us
to his authorities in support of this statement.

It appears, however, not improbable that *some* religious
house had existed on the site afterwards occupied by Rushen
Abbey, and at a date prior to 1134, from the circumstance
that in the *Chronicon Manniæ*, though mention is made of the
grant of lands in 1134, no notice occurs of the erection of buildings until 1192, when the monks transferred themselves to
Douglas for four years, during which they were engaged in
enlarging their accommodation at Rushen. The church of the
fraternity was not completed and consecrated until 1257, in
the episcopate of Richard Bishop of the Sudereys, in the fifth

year of the reign of Magnus Olaveson, when Simon was abbot.
(See *Chronicon Manniæ*, anno 1257.) We have, however, the
records of interments, within the Abbey, of several illustrious
persons prior to this last date, who were chiefly connected with
the royal family in Man. Thus Reginald, Bishop of Sodor and
Man, nephew to Olave Kleining, King of Man, was buried
here in 1225; so were King Olave Godredson (Olave the Black)
in 1237, and his son Reginald in 1248; also the Norwegian,
Jarl Gospatrick, in 1240. After this, the last Norwegian King
of Man, Magnus, was interred in the abbey in 1265.

It is not improbable that Olave Kleining himself was transferred hither after his barbarous murder by his nephew, Reginald Haroldson, at Ramsey in 1154, as there is no account
given in the *Chronicon Manniæ* of his interment elsewhere, and
the monks of that religious foundation would doubtless feel
anxious to have within the precincts of their house the body of
their chief patron.

The so-called "abbot stone" of Rushen is evidently the
coffin-lid of some military person, and of the fourteenth century, as will be seen on referring to the representation of it
given in my *Runic and other Monumental Remains of the Isle
of Man*, plate xiii, fig. 43. Its original site is not known, as
it has been shifted from time to time in the garden where it
now lies buried. It was, however, dug up for the inspection
of the members of the Cambrian Archæological Association on
the occasion of their visit in the year 1865. One would have
thought it more desirable to place it in the vaulted passage,
shortly to be mentioned, where it would be protected from the
rain; and might, if necessary, be also secured from mischievous
persons by an iron railing.

The present remains of the Abbey are in such a state that,
without an extensive exploration of foundation walls, any satisfactory assignment of its various portions seems hopeless.
The establishment must, however, have been very extensive.
There are undoubted evidences of its having been fortified.

Chaloner's drawing, made about two centuries ago, is so rude and imperfect that little more is to be learnt from it of the original arrangements, than from an inspection of the existing ruins. There were, according to the drawing, five towers, all of them pierced with square-headed openings, built of rude masonry, and exhibiting no decided architectural details. Of

these five, three alone now remain, which have been partially converted into appendages to two modern dwelling-houses. The only decided architectural detail is the plain chamfered arch given in the cut, existing in one of the towers which

formed a part of the church. Making allowance for the nature
of the building materials found on the island, and the little
progress which architecture could have made in such a remote
and inaccessible spot, it may be assigned, in spite of its older
appearance, to the period when the monks restored or rebuilt
the church, namely the middle of the thirteenth century.

A small, single light, of more doubtful date, is also here
given. It exists in the exterior face of the wall above.

At a spot which we might conclude to be the western end
of the Abbey Church, we have a remarkable portion of a
vaulted passage. It may have been simply the substructure
of some part of the domestic buildings, though there are appearances about it leading to a suspicion that it may, in some
way, have been connected with the crypt. On one of the key-

stones of the arch there are traces of a socket, from which
might have been suspended the iron hook of a corpse-light;
and it is, moreover, certain that the remains of bodies have
been found in the same spot. Here also is said to have been
the entrance to a subterranean passage leading to Rushen
Castle. To make such a passage must have caused no little
trouble to the excavators in those days, as they would have
had to tunnel through two miles of hard mountain limestone.
There are, however, few abbeys or castles without a similar
legend, and of the same amount of credibility.

A large, well-proportioned hall remains nearly intact, save a
part of one of the sides, which has been rebuilt. At first sight
it might be taken as the refectory, but was more probably intended for the use of the lay brethren or strangers.

RUINED TOWER, RUSHEN ABBEY, ISLE OF MAN.

There is also remaining one well-proportioned tower, of somewhat moderate dimensions, engaged in the curtain wall which once surrounded the monastery. On each of two of its sides, commanding the curtain, has been an opening which projected on rude but bold corbeling. (See the cut.) Whether these openings were simply windows, or intended for defence of the curtain, or even used as *latrinæ* (although the situation would in that case be singular), is a matter of doubt.

As already stated, it is by no means easy to form any opinion as to the date of these remains of the Abbey, from the absence of all safe indications, the rudeness of the material, and the scarcity of contemporaneous structures in the island. The tower at Bishop's Court, although somewhat different in proportions, is probably of the same date. Rushen Castle itself, notwithstanding the antiquity popularly assigned to it, is probably not older than the thirteenth, and more likely, is of the fourteenth, century, although its original form of a plain, square keep, before the additions to its four faces, points to the period of Newcastle and Rochester Castles. The discrepancy may be, perhaps, explained by the circumstances of its builders being Scandinavian. It has, at least, been said to bear a striking resemblance to the Castle of Elsinore.

With regard to the other ecclesiastical buildings which may have to be compared with Rushen Abbey, we may note that, whilst no portion of the Cathedral at Peel appears to be earlier than the thirteenth century, the tower and nave belong to the fourteenth. The only remaining portions of the Friary of Bechmaken, in Kirk Arbory (or Kirk Cairbre), founded by the Grey Friars in 1373, are evidently of fifteenth century work.

On the whole, it may be suggested that the remains at Rushen Abbey, or at least the greater part of them, belong to the thirteenth century. We may assign, perhaps, some small portion to the fourteenth. A few tiles have been found which are nearer the fifteenth than the fourteenth.

As to the original extent of the buildings, although not as to their age, some information may be obtained from the account of the lead, timber, slate, etc., of the Abbey sold at its dissolution, and which are given in Rolls 32, 34, 36, 37 Henry VIII, formerly at Carlton Ride, and now doubtlessly in the Record Office.

In one of the Rolls is given an interesting account of the silver plate sold to the Earl of Derby for the sum of £38 : 8 : 8 ; amongst which occur the following items, viz., "four chalices, one crouche (*i.e.*, the abbot's pastoral staff), one censer, one cross, two little headless crosses, one ship (*navicula*), one hand and one byshope's head (probably reliquaries), four cruets, eleven spoons, with two standing cups, two *pocula* (called ale-pottes) with covers, one flat *pece*, one salt, two *masers* (wooden drinking cups silver mounted), and one pix of silver."

A *computus* of the demesnes property of the Abbey, occurs in a Roll, 1540-41, a transcript of which is in the possession of Mark Quayle, Esq., the present Clerk of the Rolls in the Isle of Man, and which I had printed *in extenso* in my *Story of Rushen Castle and Rushen Abbey*. It is given below.

If, however, so little can be ascertained of the age and extent of Rushen Abbey, the same, fortunately, cannot be said of the little adjoining bridge called the "Crossag," built, no doubt, by the improving Cistercian monks. From its retired situation, fortunately, it has been spared *improvements*, or any serious alterations ; so that we have here an example of a thirteenth century bridge nearly in the same state as it was left by the builders. On account of its picturesque position at the foot of the mill-dam, which may have been raised by the Cistercians themselves, it is well worth the notice, not merely of the antiquarian, but also of the ordinary tourist. Its breadth in the centre does not exceed three feet three inches in the clear,— a space evidently pointing to times when ordinary carts were not in use.

One of the arches on the opposite side to that given in the

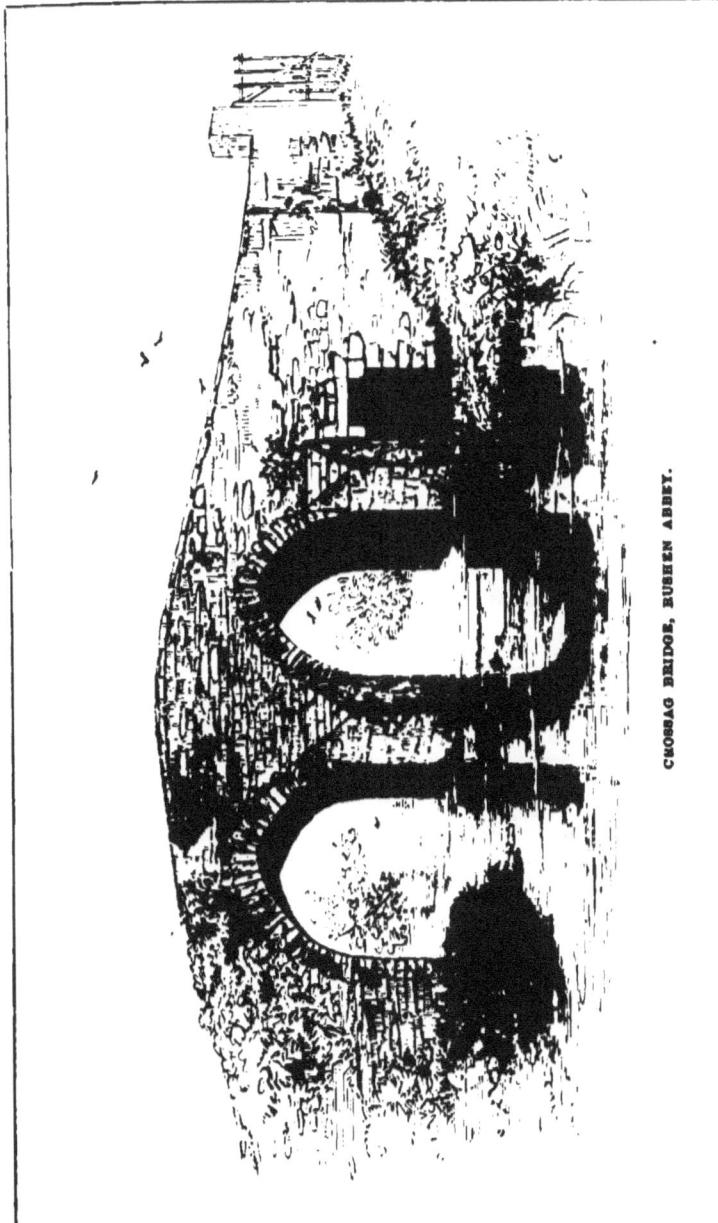

CROSBAG BRIDGE, BUSKEN ABBEY.

accompanying accurate illustration by Mr. Blight, has been subsequently repaired and a plain semicircular arch substituted for the pointed one (see plate).

At one end (the western) of the bridge will be seen a small subsidiary arch somewhat of the Caernarvon type, but an original portion of the structure. From its smallness, as well as from the material at hand, such an arrangement is so natural that it may be assigned to any time, and may well give the idea of the more regular Caernarvon (or, as it is sometimes called, the *square-headed trefoil*), which subsequently was in many cases adopted, for its appearance as well as for its convenient form. We have several doorways of this type in the Castle of Rushen.

The following is the *computus* above referred. The original is not at present to be found. Rolls of a similar nature are preserved amongst the Ministers' Accounts, with the Augmentation Office Documents, in the Record Office: viz., a Computus from April 15th to Michaelmas, 32 Henry VIII; Michaelmas, 33 Henry VIII, to the same feast 34 Henry VIII; the like accounts, 36 to 37 Henry VIII, and 37 to 38 Henry VIII; and a series of Rolls, five in number, from the accession of Edward VI to the sixth year of his reign. The original Roll, of which the portion relating to Rushen Abbey is subjoined, may have been lost at the fire at the Houses of Parliament, the records of the Augmentation Office having been at that period kept at Westminster. A portion of the Roll, as to the Demesne Lands, has been printed in Caley's edition of Dugdale's *Monasticon*, vol. v, p, 256.

Russhing nuper Monasterium \
  infra Insulam de Man.

COMPUTUS Roberti Calcott deputati prenobilis Comitis Derbie, occupatoris terrarum et possessionum ibidem, a festo

Sancti Michaelis Archangeli, anno regni Henrici, Dei gratia
Anglie, Francie, et Hibernie Regis, fidei Defensoris, ac in
terris supremi capitis Anglicane et Hibernice Ecclesie, xxxiij^{do},*
usque idem festum anno regni Regis predicti xxxiij, scilicet
per unum annum integrum.   [1540-41.]

    Arreragia nulla.   Quia primus Computus dicti Computatoris.
                     Summa nulla.

FIRMA Terrarum Dominicalium.   Sed respondet de xj. l. xvj. s.
x. d. de firma scitus nuper monasterii cum edificiis, graungiis, stabulis, ortis, pomeriis, infra preciuctum dicti nuper
monasterii existentibus, videlicet, pro firma scitus dicte nuper
domus cum edificiis, graungiis, stabulis, ortis, pomeriis, eidem
pertinentibus, continentis per estimationem j. acr. dim. iiij. s.
et uno clauso terre arrabilis vocato the Kreketts, ac uno clauso
vocato Bole Makketts continentibus per estimationem xl. acr.
xx. s. cum uno clauso vocato Garland Hill continente per estimationem xxiv. acr. xij. s. ac uno clauso vocato Wynowehill
continente per estimationem xviij. acr. ix. s. cum uno clauso
vocato Boulcton continente xxiv. acr. pasture arrabilis xij. s.
uno clauso vocato Grete Close jacente subtus Kirkmalewe ac ij.
parvis clausuris jacentibus juxta aquam in orientali parte
earumdem, continentibus per estimationem lx. acr. pasture
xxx. s. cum uno clauso vocato Dalerache continente per estimationem xxxiv. acr. pasture xij. s. uno clauso vocato Grete
Barley fielde continente per estimationem xxx. acr. pasture xv. s.
cum uno clauso vocato Depefold continente per estimationem acr.
pasture iij. s. uno clauso vocato Littill Barlefold continente per
estimationem iv. acr. ac uno clauso vocato the Cot continente
per estimationem xvj. acr. x. s. uno clauso vocato the Brome
continente per estimationem x. acr. v. s. uno clauso vocato
Reynehullett continente per estimationem viij. acr. iv. s. uno
clauso vocato the Nuttfolds, et uno clauso vocato Cotters
grounde cum campo jacente sub le Broome ac the lawe Gayre

* Sic in the transcript, probably for 32nd Henry VIII.

Skynnershill diviso in iij. clausis, continentibus per estimationem xv. acr. vii. s. vi. d. cum uno clauso vocato Stockfeld
continente per estimationem xxiv. acr. pasture arr' xij. s. uno
clauso vocato the Horse Close continente per estimationem xv.
acr. vij. s. vj. d. uno clauso vocato White Feld cum una parcella
vocata Symondos Grounde, cum una parcella vocata Corens
Grounde, cum una alia parcella de le Horse Close, continentibus per estimationem vij. acr. terre arrabilis et pasture iij. s. vj. d.
ac uno clauso vocato Grete Belownde cum una parcella prati
eidem pertinente continentibus in toto xxvj. acr. xiij. s. et uno
clauso vocato Whyuny Close cum una parva clausura continentibus in toto x. acr. v. s. ac uno clauso de Corse Meadowe
vocato Denyse Close continente per estimationem vj. acr. iij. s.
cum uno clauso vocato Littill Belownde continente per estimationem xx. acr. terr. x. s. et uno clauso vocato the Lond
Folds ajacente Skiprig, cum uno clauso vocato Calf Close, ac
cum uno alio clauso vocato Guley Felde, ac uno parcella prati
adjacentis, continentibus in toto xvj. acr. viij. s. ac cum uno
clauso vocato Skiprig continente per estimationem xx. acr.
pasture arr' x. s. ij. clausis de Corse Medowe called the Grete
Medowe continentibus per estimationem xx. acr. xx. s. et cum
uno parvo clauso jacente juxta le White Stone continente per
estimationem ij. acr. terr. xvj. d.   In toto ut supra.

Summa.   xj. £. xvj. s. x. d.

Parochia de Kirkmalewe infra Sheddinge de⎫
Russhinge.—Tenentes ad voluntatem.   ⎭

ET de xxviij. £. xiiij. s. vij. d. de Redditibus et Firmis
Tenencium ad voluntatem Domini Regis ibidem, solvendis
qualibet septimana, quantum capi potest, per collectorem voca-
tum *Le More*, ad hujusmodi recipienda assignatum, juxta anti-
quam consuetudinem Insule predicte; ita quod collecta perso-
luta foret inter festa Sancti Michaelis Archangeli.*   Videlicet,

---

* This obscure passage may be explained by the corresponding statement
in another Roll, as follows :—" De firmis tenencium ad voluntatem Domini

de Willelmo Quayle pro uno tenemento cum pertinentiis per
tempus Computi vj. s.   Johanno Brideson pro uno tenemento
ibidem per idem tempus, vj. s.   Nicholao McQuayll pro tenemento xv. s.   Marke McStoyll pro tenemento iiij. s.   De relicta Gilberti Symyn pro tenemento ix. s.   Johanne Kayecowe
pro tenemento vj. s.   Johanne Andrewe pro tenemento xij. d.
Gilberto Kewyne pro tenemento vij. s. iiij. d.   Patricco Quy-
deake pro tenemento iiij. s.   Johanno Symon pro tenemento
ix. s. vj. d.   Gybbon Gellyne pro tenemento vj. s.   Paulo
Quydeak pro tenemento iiij. s. viij. d.   Johanne Dogane pro
tenemento iij. s. iiij. d.   Johanne McQuayll pro tenemento
xv. s.   Donoldo Fergher pro tenemento vj. s.   Johanne Bell
pro tenemento xviij. d. Donold Symen et matre sua pro tenemento vj. s. iij. d.   Waltero Bell pro tenemento vj. s. iiij. d.
Johanne Taghertt pro tenemento xij. s. vj. d.   Johanne Bell
pro tenemento ix. s.   Waltero Bell pro tenemento viij. s.
Donald Brideson pro tenemento per annum ix. s.   Nelo Dog-
ham pro tenemento vj. s. viij. d.   Uxore Ricardi Brideson pro
tenemento vj. s. viij. d.   Uxore Ricardi Brideson pro tenemento ix. s.   Willelmo Andrewe pro tenemento iij. s. iiij. d.
Waltero Harrison pro tenemento x. s. viij. d.   Fynloo Makk
krollott pro tenemento iiij. s.   Thoma Harrison pro tenemento
viij. s.   Waltero Bell pro tenemento iiij. s.   Thoma McKeyn
pro tenemento vj. s. xj. d.   Relicta Finglo Fergher pro tenemento xij. s.   Johanne Brideson pro tenemento vj. s.   Fynglo
Brideson pro tenemento iiij. s. vj. d.   Waltero Taghert pro
tenemento iiij. s. vj. d.   Fynglo Bell pro tenemento iiij. s. vj. d.
Fynglo Fergher pro tenemento x. s. vj. d.   Esotto Inequisten
pro tenemento ij. s.   Johanne Andrewe pro tenemento ix. s.

Regis ibidem, solvendis per eosdem tenentes ad manus Collectoris vocati les
More, ad hoc colligendum deputati, qualibet septimana, quantum idem Col-
lector de eisdem tenentibus in qualibet septimana colligere potest, ita quod
quilibet tenens ibidem solvat totum annualem redditum suum per vel ante
festum S. Michaelis Archangeli anno 34 Regis predicti, in clauso hujus compoti accidente." *Le More*, or *The Moor*, is a Manx parish officer, whose chief
duty now is to collect waifs and estrays, deodands and escheats.

Marke Fergher pro uno tenemento ij. s. Finglo Fergher pro
uno tenemento vj. s. Reginald Harrison pro uno tenemento
xviij. s. Ricardo Fergher pro uno tenemento viij. s. Johanne
Blayno vj. s. viij. d. Relicta Roger Mackelewe pro uno tenemento iij. s. iiij. d. Edmund Mc elewe pro uno tenemento
iij. s. iiij. d. Danald Blayne pro uno tenemento vj. s. viij. d.
Johanne Brideson pro uno tenemento vj. s. viij. d. Mold Rus-
sell pro uno tenemento xij. s. Willelmo Stephenson pro uno
tenemento ij. s. Johanne McFinloo pro uno tenemento ij. s.
Patric McFayll pro uno tenemento iiij. s. Johanne Fargher pro
uno tenemento iiij. s. Willelmo Kayne pro uno tenemento
v. s. vj. d. Thoma Edwards pro uno tenemento iiij. s. Johanne
Gracye pro uno tenemento iiij. s. Johanne Quy Deake pro uno
tenemento iiij. s. Thoma Fergher pro uno tenemento v. s.
Walter Kayn pro uno tenemento vj. s. Henrico Ratcliffe pro
uno tenemento vj. s. Thoma Harrison pro uno tenemento
vj. s. Relicta Henrici Quanlye* pro uno tenemento xviij. s.
iiij. d. Jacobo Taylor pro uno tenemento v. s. Uxore Willelmi Smythe pro uno tenemento iiij. s. Reginald Barett
et Johanne Blye† pro uno tenemento v. s. Ricardo Halfall
pro uno tenemento v. s. Philippo Skylleskorn capellano
pro uno tenemento xxvij. s. vj. d. Thoma Russheton pro
tenemento cum pertinentis x. £. vj. s. viij. d. Roberto Lit-
ter Land pro tenemento et terris xxxij. s. iiij. d. Johanne
A. Moore pro tenemento et terris xxxiij. s. iiij. d. In toto
ut supra; annuatim solvendis ad festum Sancti Michaelis tantum. Et de xij. s. iiij. d. de Firma unius Molendini aquatici
Bladorum vocati Tenet‡ Lake, in tenura Laurencii Kyghley,
persolvenda ad festum Sancti Johannis Babtiste tantum. Et de
x. s. de Firma unis Molendini Bladorum Aquatici, vocati Fergher Mill, in tenura Johannis Quideake, per annum solvenda
ad festum Sancti Johannis Babtiste tantum. Et de x. s. de
Firma Molend' Bladorum Aquatici vocat' Abbay Mill, et Grag

---

* Quantyne, in another account.   ‡ Or Jenet Lake?
† Bailey, in another account.

Mill, cum uno croft oidem adjacente, in tenura Rogeri Deacon-
son, per annum solvenda ad Festum Sancti Johannis Babtisto
tantum, et tenens tenetur reparari (*sic*) in omnibus.
Summa. xxxj. £. xvj. s. xj. d.

Firma Cotagiorum de Ballasalla villa.

ET de xxxix. s. de Firma Cotagiorum in villa de Ballasalla
scituatorum, prope et juxta Monasterium predictum; videlicet,
unius cotagii in tenura Ricardi Dogan, x. d. unis cotagii in
tenura Donald Qwynno, xij. d. j. cotagii in tenura Willelmi
McQwynno, xviij. s. j. cotagii in tenura Willelmi Quidake ij. s.
j. cotagii in tenura Willelmi Smythe ij. s. j. cotagii in tenura
Ricardi Halsall iij. s. j. cotagii in tenura Johannis Fargher
viij. d. j. cotagii in tenura Nelo Bell viij. d. j. cottagii in
tenura Walteri McGarmot iij. s. j. cotagii in tenura Johannis
Glover viij. d. j. cotagii in tenura Johannis Kyrre viij. d. j.
cotagii in tenura relicto nuper Henrici Quantye xvj. d. j. cotagii in tenura Thome Mason ij. s. j. cotagii in tenura Thome
McFingloo ij. s. j. cotagii in tenura Marke Wodds viij. d. j.
cottagii in tenura Johannis Taylor ij. s. j. cotagii in tenura
Relicte David McQwayne xvj. d. j. cotagii in tenura Roberti
Kedrawe xvj. d. j. cottagii in tenura Willelmi McQuayn ij. s.
j. cotagii in tenura Stephani McKedrawo xj. d. j. cottagii in
tenura Willelmi Fergher x. d. j. cottagii in tenura Ricardi
Fisher xvj. d. j. cottagii in tenura Thome Qwynne xviij. d. j.
cottagii in tenura Mc gilhonyld iiij. s. j. cotagii in tenura
Roberti Walker xvj. d. In toto ut supra.
Summa. xxxix. s.

Parochia Sancti Germani⎫
   de Glenfaba Sheding. ⎭

ET de x. l. xix. s. v. d. de Redditibus et Firmis Tenencium
Domini Regis ad voluntatem, infra parochiam predictam.
Videlicet, Johannis Clerke pro uno tenemento cum pertinen-

ciis, ad xij.* solvendis septimanatim, quantum capi potest.
Henrici Smythe pro uno tenemento xij. Willelmi McKayne
pro tenemento xv. s. iij. d. Johannis Qwayne pro tenemento
xij. s. vj. d. Finlo McGilcroste pro tenemento vij. s. vj. d.
Donold McQwayn pro tenemento vj. s. iiij. d. Thome Howard
pro tenemento iij. s. Johannis Haliwall pro tenemento iij. s.
Relicte Johannis Mc qwayn pro tenemento iiij. s. iiij. d. Gilberti Colbyn pro uno tenemento iiij. s. iiij. d. Donald Qwhayn
pro uno tenemento iiij. s. iiij. d. Reginald McQwheyn pro uno
tenemento xviij. s. Willelmi McCayn pro uno tenemento
vij. s. iij. d. Johannis McKeyn pro uno tenemento vij. s. iiij. d.
Willelmi Stephenson pro uno tenemento xxxiij. s. iiij. d. Reginald
McCayn pro tenemento vj. s. vj. d. Johannis McGybrayce
pro tenemento vj. s. vj. d. Reginold McCayn pro uno tenemento xij. s. Willelmi McGilcrist pro tenemento iiij. s. Thome
McGilcrist pro uno tenemento ix. s. Uxoris Petri Colbyn
vj. s. vj. d. pro tenemento suo. Roberti Colbyn pro tenemento
vj. s. vj. d. Donold McQwhayn pro tenemento viij. s. j. d.
Johannis Mc qwyane pro tenemento viij. s. j. d. Hugonis
Parker pro tenemento xxij. d. In toto ut supra.

ET de xvij. s. j. d. de Redditibus et Firmis Cotagiorum in
Holme towne, in Glen faba; viz., de Richardo Ithell xx. d.
Uxore Petri Brevell iiij. d. Johanne Haworthe xvj. d. Wil-
lelmo Norias xiiij. d. Johanne Hutchon ij. d. Maryano
Hynckye ij. d. Willelmo Ascogh, xiij. d. Willelmo Kerrett iiij. d.
Roberto Alayne vij. d. Johanne Bolland iiij. d. Constabilar'
viij. d. Cristiana Inecayne xxij. d. Rogero Thompson iiij. d.
Hugone Prescote v. d. Rogero Dawson xix. d. Thoma Holland
iij. d. Recept' de le Pale xvj. d. Hugone perker ij. d. In toto
ut supra.

Summa. xj. l. xvj. s. vj. d.

Sulbye.

ET de xj. l. iiij. s. viij. d. de Redditibus et Firmis Tenencium

* *Sic*, probably xij. s. The like omission appears to occur in the following
item.

K

Domini Regis ad voluntatem ibidem, solvendis de septimana.
Videlicet, de Paulo McKrawe pro tenemento viij. s. Willelmo
McKrawe pro tenemento viij. s. Edmund McCrawe pro tenemento vj. s. Paulo McCrawe pro tenemento v. s. Huyn
Standish pro tenemento xxiiij. s. Demyster pro clausura viij. s.
viij. d. Thoma Trowthton pro tenemento iiij. s. vj. d. Gilberto
McCarro pro tenemento iiij. s. vj. d. Gilberto Gawon pro tenemento iiij. s. vj. d. Willelmo Caysmyn pro tenemento vij. s.
vj. d. Patric Cash pro tenemento v. s. viij. d. Gilberto Casy-
mound pro tenemento ij. s. Donold Kyllycorne pro tenemento
xij. s. Willelmo Kyllop pro tenemento ix. s. Paulo McKarram
pro tenemento xij. s. Johanne Thorman pro tenemento xij. s.
Willelmo McKewn ix. s. Willelmo McCashe ix. s. Patric
McKillope pro tenemento vj. s. Ricardo McKillop pro tenemento viij. s. Thoma McKillop pro tenemento vj. s. Thoma
McGarret pro tenemento vij. s. iiij. d. Willelmo McKillop pro
tenemento viij. d. Roberto McKerran pro tenemento v. s.
Edmund McKerron pro tenemento ix. s. Gilberto McOttor
pro tenemento v. s. Danold Kyllop pro cottagio xviij. d.
Marin' Ine Crayne pro cotagio vj. d. Relicta McQwyne pro
cotagio vj. d. et Baho Calyworre Ine Casso vj. d. De vj. s. de
firma unis molendini ibidem hic non respondet, eo quod jacet
vastum et inoccupatum, et nil inde levatur per tempus unis
compoti, ex sacramento computatoris. In toto ut supra.

Summa.   xj. l. iiij. s. viij. d.

Skynscowe in parochia Sancti
Lonani de Garf Sheding.

ET de lv. s. viij. d. de redditibus et firmis tenencium Domini
Regis ibidem, solvendis septimanatim. Videlicet, de Gilberto
McCloyne pro tenemento xvj. s. iiij. d. Roberto Lownye pro
tenemento xij. s. Johanne McOtter pro tenemento iij. s. vj. d.
Patric McFelys pro tenemento viij. s. iiij. d. Johanne McFelys
pro tenemento iij. s. vj. d. Donald McFelys pro cotagio xviij. d.
Gilberto Lowneye pro cotagio xiiij. d. Patrick Lownye pro

cotagio ij. s. ij. d. Johanne Lownye pro cotagio viij. d. et Willelmo Lownye pro cotagio vj. d. In toto ut supra.

Summa, lv. s. viij. d.

Spiritualitates.

Et de vij. l. vj. s. viij. d. de Firma totius Rectorie de Kirke-criste in Sheding; necnon omnium terrarum et tenementorum quorumcumque infra parochiam de Kirkecriste predictam, dicto nuper Domui pertinentium, nencon omnes et omnimodo decime allecium' except omnino et reserv' omnes et omnimodo porciones Episcopi exeuntes de Rectoria predicta, aceciam Decime j. ba-telli Domino reservat' per annum ut supra; sicut dimiss' Owino Norresse Clerico, per Identuram pro termino (*blank*) datam anno Domini M D xxv^{to}; solvend' ad Festum pasche tantum. De decimis allecium captorum infra parochiam predictam, vide-licet, de qualibet cimba xij. d., hoc anno nil, quia nulla piscaria ibidem accidebat. Et de iiij. l. xij. s. de Firma Rectorie Ec-clesie parochialis de Kirk harbary, alias de Sancto Columb, sicut dimisse Johanni Gardiner ad voluntatem Domini, tantum-modo exceptis et reservatis porcionibus Episcopi et Vicarii per annum ut supra, solvend' ad Festum Pasche tantum. Et de xvj. l. xiiij. s. de Exitibus Rectorie de Kirkmalewe nuper in manibus dicti nuper Monasterii, per annum ut supra. Et de liij. s. iiij. d. de Exitibus et proficuis Rectorie ecclesje paro-chialis de Kirke Santon per annum, ut supra, sicut nuper in manibus dicti nuper Monasterii, per tempus hujus compoti. Et de lxvj. s. viij. d. de Firma Rectorie de Kirke Iownan, in tenura Jacobi Clerke per Indenturam, ut asserit, minime adhuc visam, omnes et omnimodo proficue Rectorie, exceptis por-cionibus Episcopi et Vicarii per annum ut supra, solvend' ad Festum pasche tantum.

Summa, xxxiiij. l. xij. s. viij. d.

Summa Totalis oneris, cvj. l. ij. s. iij. d.

Feoda cum Salariis.

Idem computat in Feodis prepositorum, videlicet, *Lez Ser-*

geaunts, videlicet infra parochiam Sancti Lupi xiij. s. iiij. d. ;
Glenfaba vj. s. viij. d.; Solbye vij. s. vj. d. et Skynscowe iiij. s.;
in toto pro uno anno integro finiente in Festo Sancti Michaelis
Archangeli infra tempus hujus Compoti accidente, xxxj. s. vj. d.

Et in Sallario Capellani celebrantis infra Castellum de Cas-
tell Towne, ex antiqua Fudacione, ad liij. s. iiij. d. per annum,
videlicet, in allocacione hujusmodi per tempus hujus compoti,
liij. s. iiij. d. Et in Feodo Thome Norrisse capitalis seneschalli
Terrarum ibidem, ad lxvj. s. viij. d. per annum, videlicet in
allocacione hujusmodi, per tempus hujus compoti lxvj. s. viij. d.
Et in Feodo Thome Sainesburye occupantis officium de *la
Demester* ibidem, ad xx. s. per annum, videlicet, in allocacione
hujusmodi per tempus hujus compoti, xx. s. Et in Feodo
(*blank*) Contrarotulatoris Insule pro Factura Librorum dicta-
rum, ad xx. s. per annum, videlicet in allocacione hujusmodi
per tempus hujus Compoti, xx. s. Et in Feodo dicti Thome
Sainesburye subseneschalli terrarum et Curiarum ibidem, ad
xx. s. per annum, videlicet in persolucione hujusmodi per tempus hujus compoti, xx. s.; et in Feodo Roberti Calcott Receptoris terrarum dicti nuper Prioratus, ad liij. s. iiij. d. per
annum, videlicet, in allocacione hujusmodi per tempus hujus
compoti, liij. s. iiij. d.

            Summa. xiij. l. iiij. s. x. d.

Et in denariis in Compoto Willelmi Blithman Receptoris
Domini Regis ibidem, onerati ut pro totis denariorum summis
receptis per Thomam Comitem Derbie, de Exitibus et Reven-
cionibus Officii dicti Receptoris, ac per ipsum Thomam minime
solutis super Determinacionem hujus Compoti,—iiij.^{xx} xij. l.
xvij. s. v. d.

Summa, iiij.^{xx} xij. l. xvij. s. v. d.

Summa Allocacionum et Liberacionum predictarum cvj. l.
ij. s. iij. d.

Que Summa Correspondet Summe totali predicte.

            Et equ'.*

---

   * Probably for *equat*, or *equetur*.

(From the " Chronicon Manniæ,*" Johnstone's Translation.)*

LIMITS OF CHURCH LANDS IN THE ISLE OF MAN.

I.

This is the line that divides the king's lands from those belonging to the monastery of Russin :—It runs along the wall and ditch which is between Castleton and the Monks' Lands; it winds to the south between the Monks' Meadow and M'Ewen's farm; ascends the rivulet between Gylosen and the Monks' Lands; turns to Hentracth; goes round Hentracth and Trollo-toft along the ditch and wall; descends by the ditch and wall to the river near Oxwath; turns up the same river to a rivulet between Ar-os-in and Staina; goes down to the valley called Fanc; mounts up the ascent of the hill called Wardfell; descends to the brook Mourou; ascends from the brook Mourou along the old wall to Rosfell; descends along the same wall between Cornama and Tot-man-by; descends obliquely along the same wall between Ox-raise-herad and Tot-man-by to the river called Corna. Corna is the boundary between the king and the monastery in that quarter to the ford which lies in the highway between Thorkel's farm, otherwise Kirk Michael, and Herinstad; the line then passes along the wall which is the limit between the above-mentioned Thorkel's estate and Bally-sallach; it then descends obliquely along the same wall between Cross-Ivar-Builthan, and so surrounds Bally-sallach; it then descends from Bally-sallach along the wall and ditch to the river of Russin, as is well known to the inhabitants; it then winds along the banks of that river in different directions to the above-mentioned wall and ditch, which is the limit between the abbey land and that belonging to the castle of Russin.

II.

This is the line that divides the lands of Kirkercus from the abbey lands :—It begins at the lake at Myreshaw which is

called Hesca-nappayse; and goes up to the dry moor directly
from the place called Monenyrsana; along the wood to the
place called Leabba-ankonathway; it then ascends to Roselan
as far as the brook Gryseth; and so goes up to Glendrummy;
and proceeds up to the king's way and the rock called Carig-
eth as far as the Deep-pool; and descends along the rivulet
and Hath-aryegorman; and so descends along the river Sulaby
to the wood of Myreshaw; it incloses three islands in the lake
of Myreshaw; and descends along the old moor to Duf-loch;
and so winds along and ends in the place called Hescanakep-
page.

III.

This is the line which divides the king's lands from those of
the abbey towards Skemestor:—It begins from the entrance
of the port called Lax-a; and goes up that river in a line under
the mill to the glynn lying between St. Nicholas Chapel and
the manor of Greta-stad; it then proceeds by the old wall, as
is known to the inhabitants, along the winding declivities of
the mountains, till it comes to the rivulet between Toftar-as-
mund and Ran-curlin; it then descends to the boundaries of
the manor called Orm's-house and Toftar-as-mund, and, as is
known to the country people, descends to the sea.

MINUTES OF THE PERAMBULATION OF THE ABBEY TURBARY.

SINE ANNO.

From the north corner of Boallion Renny along an old
hedgestead to the gill near St. Mary's Well, and from the said
hedgestead to the westernmost of the three white stones on
the side of Barool in a direct line, and so down by a long slate
stone set up as a landmark, and across the old high-road by
three slate stones, and so down by the south-west corner of
the Folly Rent, and so across the new high-road at a large
slate stone on the said road, and another and a white stone on

the opposite side of the ditch to the fern hillock in the midst
of the Curragh, grown over with rushes, by a hillock of soads,
to the joining of the rivulet of Sornan Barowle and the Sbinan
Rowany, and so down the said rivulet, the Cop, near Barool
Mill, and so along the said Cop adjoining Keon Dhowag, and
joining Kirk Patrick at Keon Dhowag, and so along the same
as far as the same Oxloads, and then along the pathway according to a boundary of the parishes, passing by a great stone
opposite to Keon Slew Curragh, so to the south-west corner
of Curragh Potmine at two stones there fixed, and so along
the ditch and the edge of Pot-mine Curragh, joining Kirk
Marown to the north-east corner of Rensheant land, and along
the Cop from the said corner to Pot-mine rivulet, and so
along the rivulet to the corner of Bulla Nicholas Rent, and
along the same to Shen Valley, and including Ton Vane's, the
Bolt Dallys to Monoul Gate, and so adjoining the Largy Intack,
and so along the corner of Ballin Renny aforesaid.

V.

ROBERT THE BRUS BEFORE RUSHEN CASTLE.

BY THE REV. J. G. CUMMING, M.A., F.G.S.

In the *Chronicon Manniæ et Insularum*, written by the monks of Rushen Abbey in the Isle of Man (see vol. iv, Manx Society, p. 195), there occurs this entry under date A.D. 1313 :—

" Dominus Robertus rex Scociæ applicuit apud Ramsa, videlicet, octo decimo die Maii cum multitudine navium et die dominica sequenti transivit ad Moniales de Dufglas ubi pernoctavit; et die Lunæ sequenti fecit obsessionem circa castrum de Russin, quod castrum dominus Dungawi Macdowal tenuit contra prædictum dominum regem usque diem Martis proximam post festum Sancti Barnabæ Apostoli proximo sequenti, et ipso die dictus dominus rex dictum castellum adquisivit."

It may be worth while to inquire what brought Robert the Brus on this distant expedition to Rushen Castle, and who was this " dominus Dungawi Macdowal" who held the fortress against him for more than three weeks, viz., from May the 18th to June 11th. The answer to the latter question gives, as I think, the key to the former.

This Dungawi Macdowal (called in Camden's copy of the *Chronicon Manniæ* Dingawy, Dowil, and in the *Annals of Ulster* "the Lord Donegal O'Dowill") was Duncan Macdougal, or Duncan de Ergadia. He was the second son of Alaster de Ergadia, Thane of Glasserie and Knapdale, and Lord of Lorn. He is called by Chalmers " the most illustrious Celtic chief in Galloway." He had made his escape to the Isle of Man with

a great number of Gallovidians, in order to avoid the hostility
of Robert the Brus, who was following up his attacks upon
the Comyn family, with whom the Ergadias were closely connected, in their Gallovidian territories. (See *Calendar of
Ancient Charters in the Tower of London*, p. 121.) On his
father's side he was descended from Shomhairle (or Somerled)
Mac Gilbert, Thane of Argyle, by his second wife, Affreca, an
illegitimate daughter of Olave Kleining, king of Man. His
mother was the third daughter of John the first Red Comyn,
by Marian, daughter of Alan, Lord of Galloway, and sister to
Devorgille. He was thus (like the Comyns) descended on
the female side from David Earl of Huntingdon, though his
grandfather, the first Red Comyn, founded *his* claim to the
Scottish throne by descent from Hexilda, grandaughter of
Donald Bane, king of Scotland. He was also third cousin to
Mary, daughter of Eugene de Ergadia, Lord of Lorn, and wife
of Reginald, king of Man, and afterwards Countess of Strathern.
A son of this Mary, viz., Malise, Earl of Strathern, married
Egidia Comyn, daughter of Alexander Comyn, Earl of Buchan,
and granduncle to this Duncan Macdougal. (See vol. x, Manx
Society, Appendices B and D.)

Hence he was not only closely united to the Comyns, the
great competitors with Robert the Brus for the crown of
Scotland, but had also a personal interest in the Isle of Man
by his connexions with its ancient kings. It should also be
noticed that it was a John Comyn (probably the second Red
Comyn, cousin to this Duncan de Ergadia, or Duncan Macdougal) who conquered the Isle of Man for the Scots at the
battle of Ronaldsway in 1270 (according to the *Chronicon Manniæ* 1275). To which we may add that Isabella Beaumont,
eldest daughter and coheir of Alexander Comyn, Earl of
Buchan and Lord of Whitwic in Leicestershire, was at this
time (1313) actually Queen of Man; her husband, Henry de
Beaumont, having in the previous year (1312) obtained a
grant of the island and its regalities for life from King Ed-

ward II of England. (See vol. x, Manx Society, p. 98, and
Appendix D.) John de Ergadia, the elder brother of this
Duncan, held large possessions in the Isle of Man, from which,
in consequence of the capture of Rushen Castle by Robert the
Brus, he was driven out, and he did not recover them till
1340.

The Isle of Man, then, was evidently at this time the strong-
hold of the Ergadias and the Comyns,—a kind of rallying
point to the most formidable enemies of the new dynasty. It
was, therefore, of extreme importance to Robert that he should
gain possession of it, and place it in the hands of those upon
whom he could rely. Hence we find, immediately afterwards,
that a charter was granted to Thomas Randolph, Earl of
Moray, to hold the Isle of Man under Robert the Brus. (*Rot.
Orig. in Curia Scaccarii.*)

After the foul murder of the second Red Comyn, in the
church at Dumfries, in 1307, his success at Bannockburn enabled the Brus so to waste the heritage of the Comyns " that,"
says a chronicle of the age, " of a name which numbered at
one time three earls and more than thirty belted knights,
there remained no memorial in the land, save the orisons of
the monks of Deir." ' The Ergadias seem to have been more
fortunate; and though Duncan was driven from Rushen Castle,
and his brother John at the same time lost his Manx possessions, after a series of years they returned to the family; and
it is somewhat remarkable that a descendant of John de Ergadia, Patrick Cuninghame, Esq., H.K., should at the present
time be in possession of property which almost overlooks the
Castle of Rushen.

Looking at the strength of Rushen Castle as it now stands,
we can hardly believe that it was the same as that which was
taken by Robert the Brus in three weeks. Its architecture
seems to point to the time of the first three Edwards. There
are several square-headed trefoil doorways of the thirteenth
century type; but it is probable that its main features received

their impress in the middle of the fourteenth century. The ground plan of the keep may, however, have been of an earlier and Norwegian date. It has plainly received many subsequent modifications. The glacis is said to have been made under the directions of Cardinal Wolsey, who was one of the guardians of Edward Earl of Derby and Lord of Man, *temp.* Hen. VIII, Ed. VI, Mary, and Elizabeth. James, the famous seventh Earl of Derby, made additions to the Castle in 1645; and several unsightly buildings have been joined on to the keep within the last twenty-five years. It is much to be desired that an accurate ground plan of the Castle and precincts should be made.

VI.

ANCIENT CHURCHES OF THE ISLE OF MAN, PRIOR TO THE MIDDLE AGES.

BY J. R. OLIVER, M.D.

ECCLESIASTICAL HISTORY.

AMONG the group of islands known in former times as the Sud-reyjar, stands prominently the Isle of Man. Anciently called by the various names of Mona, Menavia, Eubonia, etc., and at a later period Mannin, or the Island of Man, this small spot lying in the Irish Sea, and centrally situated as respects the neigh-bouring shores, presents very peculiar and remarkable charac-teristics. Though of insignificant geographical dimensions, being little more than thirty miles in length, and barely twelve in breadth, it is rich in historic and archæological associations. Formerly a kingdom, and to this day almost an independent country, having its own parliament, making its own laws, and regulating its own domestic affairs, it presents the singular spectacle of an island in the nineteenth century, in the heart of the British dominions, retaining Scandinavian ceremonies*

* In proof of this, I may adduce the existence of the "House of Keys", anciently called the *Taxiaxi*, and the ceremonies of the *Thingavöllr*, or Tyn-wald Hill. During the Danish occupancy of the island under the Orrys, the "House of Keys" is said to have consisted of twenty-four members, eight of which were elected by the *Sudreyjar*, or "out isles", and sixteen by the Isle of Man. The "out isles" were, *Icolmkill, Colonsay, Jura, Isla, Lewis, Arran, Bute,* and the *Cumbrays*. At this period, and also up to the close of the Nor-wegian dynasty in 1265, the Manx parliament was a representative body elected by the people; a distinctive feature, probably lost in the troublesome times succeeding the Scottish occupancy of the island under Alex. III.

and usages, long after they have ceased to exist in the land of their birth.

From a very early epoch, the Isle of Man had been the seat of a monarchial government. Its first line of kings* were princes from North Wales, who ruled over it for the space of four centuries. The earliest and most celebrated of these was Maelgwyn, King of North Wales, and nephew of the famous King Arthur. He conquered the island A.D. 525, chiefly through the assistance of his uncle. From this circumstance he received the name of *Draco Insularis*, and became one of the Knights of the Round Table. The Welsh line of kings terminated with the demise of Anarawd ap Roderic in the year 913. During this long period, a close friendship existed between the Welsh, and the Manx people, cemented and strengthened by frequent intercourse with each other. Prior to the Cambrian dynasty, a mythological character called *Mannanan Beg Mac Y Leir*, is said to have governed the Isle of Man, and to have been its first legislator or ruler. Who this personage was, or from whence he came, is not very certain. According to the most approved tradition, he was of royal extraction, and descended from one of the kings of Ireland. Being of a restless roving disposition, he found his way to Man and settled there. Unfortunately, "little Mannanan", *Mannanan beg*, as he is called in the Manx language, has the ominous character of a paynim and necromancer, who by his occult arts enveloped the island in a perpetual mist, so that strangers were unable to visit it, whilst he sat at home in ease on the top of a high mountain called Barrule.†

* For some of these see the *Annales Cambriæ*, and the *Brut y Tywysogion*.
† At this period also dwelt in Man another celebrated character called Melinus, possessed of the art of aeromancy, and likewise the secret of flying. By the latter means he could transport himself to any place he pleased in an incredible short space of time. Whether Melinus inhabited the island anterior to Mac Leir, or accompanied him to it, is uncertain; but tradition points to priority of residence on the part of Melinus. If so, the likelihood is, he was the working Vulcan who *mystified* the island, whilst Mac Leir ruled it. All Melinus's accomplishments, however, were of no avail against

The probability is, if such a person as Mannanan ever existed, he was simply some adventurous seaman or trader who, happening to visit the Isle of Man, settled in it, and made it the country of his adoption. He was there at the time of St. Patrick's visit, and whatever his skill in the occult arts may have been, it was not potent enough to prevent his banishment by the Irish Apostle. The religion of the Manx at this period is supposed to have been Druidism, and like Melinus, they were said to be addicted to the practice of the black arts, a circumstance which sorely grieved St. Patrick, so, that instead of proceeding on his journey, he stayed in the island until he had converted them from the error of their ways.

Whatever may be the amount of truth mixed up with the legend of Mac Leir, there can be little doubt that after the Roman edict, the Druids of Anglesey fled to, and found refuge in, the Isle of Man.* Here they erected their altars, disseminated their doctrines, and finally perished,—exterminated it is said by the orders of St. Patrick. At one time they must have existed in considerable numbers, instanced by the numerous places still called after them. To the present day, the peasantry use the term Druid, or Druidical, when speaking of any old ruin of whose history they have no knowledge, legendary or otherwise, and apply it alike to the stone circle of the Norseman, and the *débris* of a ruined chapel.

Insular tradition, as we see from the above, in its ascription to St. Patrick of the conversion of the Manx people, hints, that he made short work of the business, inasmuch as he destroyed the Druids by fire and sword. For the sake of St. Patrick's Christianity, however, we hope the traditionary account is not true, and we may safely ignore it, as being wholly

the great St. Patrick; for in one of his volitatorial excursions the saint winged him with a long prayer, which tumbled the magician to earth, and killed him. So says Jocelinus.

* Anderson says it was Finan, King of Scotland, who introduced Druidism into the Isle of Man, about 134 years before the Christian era (Roy. Geneal.) Upon what authority he makes this statement does not appear.

contrary to the well-known precepts and practices of the early
missionaries. They in fact did no violence to the prejudices
and feelings of our heathen ancestors; but, by judicious manage-
ment, gentleness, and kindness, won over the sympathies of
the inhabitants to the new faith. By this means only did they
establish Christianity, and firmly plant it in the affections of
the people.

Before entering upon the ecclesiological history of the Isle
of Man as developed in its numerous ruined churches, it will
be advisable to glance at its first evangelisation, and the persons who were instrumental in accomplishing it. According
to the generally received tradition, it was Christianised by St.
Patrick whilst on his journey from Rome to Ireland, about the
year 444. This opinion is founded on the authority of Jocelinus of Furness, who in his chapter entitled, "De Mannia et
aliis insulis ad Deum conversis, states, that St. Patrick returning* to Ireland, touched at the islands of the sea, one of which,
Eubonia,† that is, Man, at that time subject to Britain, by his
miracles and preaching converted to Christ". Whether St.
Patrick ever visited the Isle of Man, as stated by Jocelinus, is
open to doubt, as we find writers of equal authority with the
Furness chronicler denying that such was the case, though
they allow his influence may have had considerable weight in
effecting the changes ascribed to him. Colgan, in his *Acta
Sanctorum*, reiterates the statement of Jocelinus, that the Irish

* "Regnavignans Hiberniam, ad insulas maris convertendas devertit à
quibus Euboniam, id est, Manniam, tunc quidem Britanniæ subjectam salu-
tari prædicatione, ac Signorum exhibitione ad Christum convertit."—Jocel.,
Vita Patricii, c. xcii, f. 43.

† *Eubonia*. Aliquando Eubonia, etc. Ita Gildæ Jocelino, aliisque passim
Britannicis, et Hibernicis scriptoribus vocatur. Mannia enim prisco ser-
mone Hibernico *Eumhoin* vel *Eubhoin* appellata reperitur, ut constat ex
veteri, et eleganti carmine panegyrico, quod in laudem magni filii Godredi
Manniæ regis ante annos quingentos composuit Arthulius, sive sæculi præs-
tantissimus Poëta; quodque ponos me extat. Ibi enim Manniam sæpius
vocat *Eumhoin* abhlach, id est, pomo arbore abundans, ad distinctionem
alterius Euboniæ seu Eumoniæ, quæ cælebris olim erat sedes regum Ultoniæ,
et *Eamhain* seu *Eabhoin* mhacha Hiberni appellatur. [Actt. Sanc. Colgani.]

Apostle did visit and Christianise the island, adding, that anciently it was a dependency of Ireland, and called *Inis Patrick*,
or Patrick's Island, in honour of the Saint. Probus,* however,
a writer of the tenth century, says, that Conindrius and Romulus,
and not St. Patrick, were the first preachers of the Gospel in
Evania or Man. His words are, "Qui primi docuerunt verbum
Dei et baptismum in Evania, et per eos conversi sunt homines
insulæ ad Catholicam fidem". In the Trias Thaumaturga,†
they are called Conderius and Romailus, but it is silent as to
the conversion by St. Patrick, though it hints at the island
having become famous as a retreat for monks shortly after his
arrival in Ireland, " venit autem (Macaldus in Manuiam sive
Eubonian, olim Druidum et gentilium vatum) postea ab ad-
ventu Sancti Patricii, christi mystarum et monachorum secessu
et sede nobilem clarumque insulam".‡ According to the Tri-
partite Life, Conderius and Romailus visited the island prior
to 455, and were the persons who disseminated and propagated
the faith and doctrine of Christ in it.

These conflicting statements render it difficult to arrive at a
satisfactory conclusion as to the men by whose exertions the
Isle of Man really was Christianised, though there can be little
doubt it was by the same missionaries, or their immediate successors, who carried the Gospel to the Irish. The account
handed down to us by the foregoing chroniclers is by no means
improbable. It shows at least, that incidental visits were made
to the island by religious men, as early as the fifth century,
through whose labours a Christian church was established in a
heathen land, in the midst of an idolatrous and superstitious
people. Another difficulty meets us, respecting the identity of
the first bishop appointed to govern the new church. Jocelinus says—"he was a wise and holy man named Germanus, who
placed his 'episcopal seat', *episcopalem sedem*, in a certain pro-
montory which to this day is called St. Patrick's Isle, because

* Vita Patricii, l. ii, c. 11.
† Trias. Thau., l. iii, c. 61.   ‡ Ibid.

he had remained there for some time.* The site of this seat
or place of worship was old Jurby Church, now beneath the
waves.   Here, says the same authority, St. Patrick landed on
his return from visiting the islands of the sea, "ad insulas
maris", and established a central station for missionary operations, which he placed under the pastoral charge of St. German,† enjoining him to build chapels and churches to strengthen
and confirm the people in the faith.   Jocelinus is the only
writer among the mediæval historians, who asserts the Manx
episcopacy of this prelate, an error clearly fallen into through
the profundity of his legendary attainments.   The Chronicon
Manniæ, a better authority, is silent as to Germanus having
been Bishop of Man, an omission its authors would not have
been guilty of, had such been the case.   From this it is evident
that the Furness chronicler has committed the mistake of con-
founding the missions of Palladius and St. German with the
apostleship of St. Patrick, an error the more remarkable in
this celebrated writer, as he must have been well acquainted
with the object and extent of the Bishop of Auxerre's visit to
England.   Jocelinus, however, is borne out in his statement
respecting the Manx episcopacy by insular tradition, which not
only fully supports him, but ascribes to this bishop the foundation of the numerous small chapels scattered throughout the
island, called *Cabbals*, *Keeills*, and *Treen Churches*.   Nevertheless, for the reasons given above, we are compelled to reject
both the Manx tradition and the narrative of Jocelinus as

* " S. Patricius virum sanctum et sapientem, Germanum nominatum, in
episcopum promotum, illius gentis ecclesiæ novellæ regentem præposuit, et
in quodam promontorio, quod adhuc insula Patricii dicitur, eo quod ipse
ibidem aliquantulum demorabatur, et episcopalem sedem posuit."—*Vita
Patricii*, c. xcii, f. 43.

† *Germanus*. Vide de ipso Martyrol. Tamlacten. Marianum Gorm. et
Cathaldum Maguir ad 30 Julii. [Act. Sanc.] Butler, in his lives of the
Saints, mentions three bishops of this name. *St. Germanus*, Bishop of
Auxerre, C.; born A.D. 380; died July 26, A.D. 448. *St. Germanus*, Bishop
of Capua; legate 519; died October 30, A.D. 510. *St. Germanus*, Bishop
of Paris; died May 28, A.D. 576.

F

untenable, and seek in another quarter the founder of our ecclesiastical system.

Unfortunately, much confusion has arisen in consequence of
the difficulty of identifying the traditionary Germanus of the
Isle of Man, with any real person. We have seen he could not
have been the famous Bishop of Antissiodorum (Auxerre),
as this prelate's first visit to England was in 429, fifteen years
before the supposed advent of St. Patrick in Man; and his
last, A.D. 448, just four years afterwards.* There are, however,
two others bearing the same name, who flourished towards the
close of St. Patrick's life; but, as neither were bishops, they
do not lessen the perplexity. One of these, mentioned by Ca-
nisius, and also by Messingham,† in his life of Adamnan, was a
Christian bard; and the other is described as a monk belonging to the monastery of St. Finnian, under whom St. Columba
studied.‡ The only feasible explanation seems to be, that in
course of time, the Bishop of Auxerre's substantiality became
incorporated into a mythical personage, and so gave rise to the
Manx tradition.§

The historic fact then amounts to this, that as it is wholly
impossible that Germanus could at any time have been Bishop
of Man, the only remaining person to whom we can have recourse with any degree of probability is St. Maughold, variously
called Maccaldus, Macfail, Maguil, and Cyclops.|| He was one
of St. Patrick's earliest converts in Ireland, and was most
likely sent to the island to assist in the work of its conversion.
Ultimately, he attained to the episcopal degree,¶ and built the
church near Ramsey called after him. He must have been an
active and zealous labourer in his new sphere, as he has an
extraordinary reputation for sanctity and miraculous endow-

---

* Baron. Ann., A.D. 429.   † Lib. 3, c. 4.   ‡ Vit. S. Kieran., c. 32.
§ There is a see of St. German in Cornwall.
|| So nicknamed in the *Fourth Life* from having only one eye, p. 45, Sec. lxxxi.
¶ " Hic enim Maccaldus est episcopus et antistes clarus *Ardebnanensis*"
(Hill of Evania, or Man) " cujus nos suffragia adjuvent sancta."—*Tr. Thau.*,
Septima Vita. p. 161, Sec. lxi.

ments—gifts very abundant in those days, but remarkably scarce
now. It is to be regretted that so little is known of his career.
He lived in an age when annalists were few, and monastic es-
tablishments yet in their infancy, so that if any biographies
were written, they must have perished in the inroads of the
Danes and Norwegians into this island. The few passing
notices we find of him in the *Chronicon Manniæ*, and other
sources, add little to our knowledge beyond the increase of our
legendary lore, and an accession to the treasury of ridiculous
miracles which the biographers of the middle ages so delighted
to record.

The following account of St. Maughold from the Book of
Armagh, is the oldest in existence. It is said to have been
written about the middle of the seventh century. The Latin
text is given below for the benefit of those who may wish to
possess the original.

There was a certain man in the country of the *Ulothores*
(? Ulster), in the time of St. Patrick, *Maccuil* of Macugrecca,
and this man was very impious, most cruel, tyrannical, so that he
was called Cyclops* by the more thoughtful, depraved in words,
in words intemperate, malignant in action, bitter in spirit,
quarrelsome in disposition, abandoned in body, cruel in mind, a
heathen in life, and void of conscience. Sunk into such a depth

LIBER ARDMACHÆ.† VITA S. PATRICII.

Erat quidam homo in regionibus Ulothorum Patricii tempore Maccuil Macugreccæ et erat hic homo valde impius sævus
tyrannus ut Cyclops nominaretur cogitantioribus,

* "*Cyclops nominaretur.*" Hic est Demana episcopus. Qui ab authore
vitæ præcedentis Maguil a Probo Lib. 2, c. 9, Macfil, a Jocelino, c. 151 et
152, auth. op. Trip., p. 3, c. 60. Machaldus; hic nunc Cyclops, nunc Demana, sed duplici ut videtur, cognomento appellatur. Cyclops enim ad
similitudinem Polyphemi, Cyclopis, ob magna latrocinia et scelera, famosi,
vocatur. Item, *Demana*, nisi *de Mona* potius, sive *de Nannia* sit legendum,
quia dæmon Hibernis etiam Denham appellatur.

† The text, which was very corrupt, is here emended.

of impiety, that on a certain day, sitting in a rough and high
mountainous place, viz., *Hindruim Maccuechach*, where he daily
exercised his tyranny, committing the greatest enormities, slay-
ing his guests on their journey with abandoned cruelty and cruel
wickedness; seeing also St. Patrick shining in the clear light of
faith, sparkling with a certain wonderful glory of the diadem of
the heavenly country, firm in the unshaken confidence of his doctrine, walking in a way suitable to his life, him he meditated to
slay, saying to his attendants, "Behold this seducer and perver-
ter of men comes, whose custom is to practise deceits to entrap
many men, and to seduce them; let us go, therefore, and tempt
him; and let us know if that God in whom he glories has any
power."

And they tempted the holy man, they tempted him in this .
way, they placed one of themselves under a cloak, feigning him
to be lying in the agony of death, that they might try the Saint

pravus	verbis	In tantum
verbis	intemperatus	vergens impietati
factis	malignus	in profundum
spiritu	amarus	ita ut die
anima	iracondus	quadam
corpore	sceleratus	in montoso
mente	crudelis	aspero alto
vita	gentilis	quo sedens
conscientia	inanis	loco

Hindrium Maccuechach, ubi ille tyrranidem cotidie exercebat,
Diberca signa sumens, nequissima crudelitate et transeuntes
hospites crudeli scelere interficiens; Sanctum quoque Patricium
claro fidei lumine radiantem, et mira quadam cœlestis patriæ
gloria diadematæ fulgentem videns, eum, inconcussa doctrinæ
fiducia, per congruum vitæ iter ambulantem, interficere cogi-
taret, dicens satelitibus suis, ecce seductor ille et perversor
hominum venit cui mos facere præstigias ut decipiat homines
multosque seducat eamus ergo et temptemus eum et sciemus
si habet potentiam aliquam ille Deus in quo se glorietur.

by this kind of deception ; so, on the arrival of St. Patrick with his disciples, they were having recourse to tricks, muttering prayers and practising witchcraft and incantations. The heathen said to him, " Behold one of us is now sick : approach, therefore, and chaunt some of the incantations of your sect over him, if perchance he may be healed."

St. Patrick, knowing all their stratagems and deceits, with firmness and intrepidity, said, " It would be no wonder if he had been sick ;" and, his companions uncovering the face of him feigning sickness, saw that he was now dead ; and, the heathens, amazed and astonished at such a miracle, said among themselves, " Truly this man is from God ; we have done evil in tempting him."

But, St. Patrick having turned to Maccuil, says, " Why did you seek to tempt me ?" The cruel tyrant answered, " I am sorry for what I have done ; whatever you command me I will perform, and I now deliver myself into the power of your

Temptaveruntque virum sanctum, in hoc modo temptaverunt, posuerunt unum ex semetipsis sanum in medio eorum sub sago jacentem infirmitatemque mortis simulantem, ut probarent sanctum, in hujusque modi fallere sanctum seductorem virtutis præstigias et orationes veneficia vel incantationes nominantes ; adveniente Sancto Patricio cum discipulis suis, gentiles dixerunt ei, ecco unus ex nobis nunc infirmitatus est, accede itaque et canta super eum aliquas incantationes sectæ tuæ si forte sanari posset.

Sanctus Patricius sciens omnes doles et fallacias eorum, constanter et intrepide ait, nec mirum si infirmis fuisset; et revelantes socii ejus faciem insimulantis infirmitatem, viderunt eum jam mortuum ; at illi obstupescentes admirantesque tale miraculum dixerunt intra se gentes vere hic homo Dei est malefecimus temptantes eum.

Sanctus vero Patricius conversus ad Maccuil ait, quare temptare me voluisti, responditque ille tyrannus crudelis ait pœni-

Supreme God, whom you preach." And the saint said, " Believe, therefore, in my God, the Lord Jesus, and confess your
sins, and be baptised in the name of the Father, and of the
Son, and of the Holy Spirit." And he was converted in that
hour, and believed in the Eternal God, and, moreover, was
baptised ; and then Maccuil added this saying, " I confess to
thee, my holy Lord Patrick, that I proposed to kill you. Judge,
therefore, how much I owe for so great a crime." Patrick
said, " I am not able to judge, but God will judge."

" Do you, therefore, depart now unarmed to the sea, and
pass over quickly from this country, Ireland, taking nothing
with you of your substance, except a small common garment
with which you may be able to cover your body, eating nothing
and drinking nothing of the fruit of this island, having a mark
of your sins on your head, and when you reach the sea bind
your feet together with an iron fetter, and cast the key of
it into the sea, and set out in a boat of one hide, without

teat me facti hujus et quodcumque perceperis missi faciam et
trado me nunc in potentiam Dei tui excelsi quem prædicas. Et
ait Sanctus, crede ergo in Deo meo Domino Jesus et confitere
peccata tua et baptizare in nomine Patris et Filii et Spiritus
Sancti. Et conversus in illa hora credidit Deo eterno baptizat-
usque est; insuper et nunc addidit Maccuil dicens, confiteor tibi
Sancte domine, mi Patricii, quia proposui te interficere, judica
ergo quantum debuerit pro tanto ac tali crimine, et ait Patricius,
non possum judicare sed deus judicabit.

Tu tunc egredere nunc inermis ad mare et transi velociter de
regione hoc hibernensi, nihil tollens tecum de tua substantia
præter vile et parvum instrumentum quo possit corpus tuum
contegi, nihil gustans nihilque bibens de fructu insulæ hujus,
habens insigne peccati tui in capite tuo, et postquam per-
venias ad mare, conliga pedes tuos conpede ferreo et projice
clavim ejus in mari et mitte te in navim unius pellis absque
gubernaculo et absque remo, et quocumque te duxerit ventus

rudder or oar, and wherever the wind and sea shall lead you, be prepared to remain, and to whatever land Divine Providence shall carry you, be prepared to live there and obey the Divine commands."

And Maccuil said, "I will do as you have said; but, respecting the dead man, what shall we do?" And Patrick said, "He shall live, and shall rise again without pain." And Patrick restored him to life in that hour, and he revived quite sound.

And Maccuil departed thence very speedily to the sea. The right side of the plain of Inis is reached, having his confidence unshaken in the faith, and binding himself on the shore, casting the key into the sea, according to what was commanded him, he then embarked in a little boat, and the north wind arose and bore him to the south, and cast him on the island called Evonia, and he found there two men very wonderful in faith and doctrine who first taught the word of God and baptism in Evonia.

And the men of the island were converted by their doctrine

et mare, esto paratus, et terram in quamcunque deferet te divina providentia, inhabita et exerce tibi divina mandata.

Dixitque Maccuil sic faciam ut dixisti divine, autem mortuo quid faciemus? et ait Patricius vivet et exsurget sine dolore, et suscitavit eum Patricius in illa hora, et revixit sanus.

Et migravit inde Maccuil tam cito ad mare. Dexterum campi Inis habetur fiducia inconcussa fidei, collegansque se in litore jeciens clavim in mare, secundum quod præceptum est ei, ascendit mare in navicula, et inspiravit illi ventus aquilo et sustulit eum ad meridiem jecit que eum in insulam Evoniam nomine invenitque ibi duos viros valde mirabiles, in fide et doctrina fulgentes, qui primi docuerunt verbum Dei et baptismum in Evonia.

Et conversi sunt homines insulæ in doctrina eorum ad fidem catholicam quorum nomina sunt Conindri et Rumili.* Hii vero

* *Coindrius* et *Romulus*. Fuit uterque Patricii discipulus, et Manniæ successive episcopus, ut de eis scribunt Joc., c. 152. Prob., Lib. 2, c. 10, et

to the Catholic faith, whose names are Conindrus and Rumilus. But these, seeing a man of the same habit, wondered and pitied him, and lifting him out of the sea, the spiritual fathers received him with joy. He, therefore, after finding himself in a region, believing in God, conformed himself body and soul to their guidance, and spent the remainder of his life with those two holy bishops till he was appointed their successor in the bishopric.

This is Maccuil Dimane,* Abbot and Bishop of Arddæ Huimdonii.†

videntes virum unius habitus mirati sunt, et miserti sunt illius elevaveruntque de mari, suscipientes cum gaudio, ille igitur, ubi inventi sunt spirituales patres in regione a Deo sibi credita, ad regulam eorum corpus et animum exercuit, et totum vitæ tempus exegit apud eos duos sanctos episcopos, usque dum successor eorum in episcopatu effectus est.

Hic est Maccuil Dimane episcopus et antistes Arddæ Huimnonii.

The following addition to the above is from the Triadis Thaumaturgæ of Colgan. It is the same as given by Jocelinus, in his life of St. Patrick, and lends additional interest to the life of St. Maughold, as narrated in the Book of Armagh.

auth. oper. Prip. et Ussero in indice chron. ad an. 474, ut hic Romulus vocatur ejus condiscipuli, et collegæ Conindrii, sive rectius Condirii, ordinationem refert. Usserus in predictum an. 474.   Condirii natalis celebratur die 17 Nov., juxta Mart. Tamlact. et Mariani; Romuli verò 18 Nov., juxta Ferrar in Catal. generali dicentem ; in Hibernia S. Romuli episcopi; et in notis, Romuli alias Romani ex Martyroiogio Subensi, de eo Joc., c. 152. Martyrologium Subensi, quod citat ita loquitur 14 Kal. Decemb. in Hibernia S. Romani episcopi et confessoris, Romani etiam, uti et Romani ad eundem diem meminit Marian Gorm. (Trias Thaum.)

A.D.—88. Conindrio et Romulo, St. Patricii discipulis, et Manniæ insulæ episcopis vita functis, St. Maguil sive Machaldus, St. Patricii etiam discipulus, successit. (Vita S. Gildæ Badonici, p. 190; Colgan's Actta Sanctorum.)

* Isle of Man. Intended for *De Mannia.*

† The Irish Latinised form of Eubonia; *i. e., Arddæ Eumhonia,* Hill of Eubonia, or Man.

"And when he had for some time abided there, a fish was one day taken in the sea, and brought into their dwelling, and when the fish was opened before them, a key was found in his belly, and Machaldus being released from his chains, gave thanks unto God, and went thenceforth free;* and he increased in holiness, and after the decease of these holy bishops, attained to the episcopal degree, and being eminent in his miracles and in his virtues, there did he rest. In that island was a city called after him, of no small extent, the remains of whose walls may yet be seen. And in the cemetery of its church is a

"Qui cum in illo loco multo tempore demoraretur, die quadam piscis in pelago captus, ad ejus hospitium deportabatur, qui cum coram illo incideretur, clavis in ejus intestinis inveniebatur, qua compedibus admota et immissa illorum claustrum referatur; ipseque solatus Deo gratias multiplices agens, libor gradiebatur. Qui postmodum in magna sanctitate excrescens, post decessum Sanctorum Episcoporum prædictorum Episcopalem gradum promeruit, signis et virtutibus clarus, ibidem requievit.† Habebatur enim in illa insula civitas quondam non exigua, cujus murorum adhuc cernuntur residua, ex ejus nomine

* This part of the legend is evidently borrowed from the Talmudists' fable of Asàf and Sakhar, which runs as follows:—
"King Solomon one day whilst bathing, entrusted his signet ring for safe keeping to his concubine Amina. She, whilst in charge of the jewel, was visited by a demon of the name of *Sakhar*, in the likeness and form of Solomon, who thus obtained the ring. The consequence was, that *Sakhar* became possessed of the kingdom for the space of forty days; whilst Solomon, changed in appearance and reduced to beggary, was obliged to wander about and solicit alms for subsistence. When the forty.days had expired, the demon threw the king's signet into the sea, when it was swallowed by a fish. The fish was caught a short time afterwards and given to Solomon, who, on opening it, found his ring in the belly. He thus recovered his kingdom, and having seized *Sakhar*, caused a great stone to be fastened to his neck and cast into the Lake of Tiberias." (Talm. En. Jacob, part 2.)

† "*Ibidem requievit*", acta ejus breviter perstringit Jocelinus, cap. 15, et 152 vitæ S. Patricii, et agunt de eo ad 25 Aprilis, S. Ængussius, Marian. Gorm. et Martyrologio Tamlactensi ad quem diem nos ejus vitam dabimus. (Colgan's Actt. Sanc.)

sarcophagus of hollow stone, out of which a spring continually
exudes, nay, freely floweth, which is sweet to the palate,
wholesome to the taste, and healeth divers infirmities, and the
deadliness of poison; for whoso drinketh thereof, either re-
ceiveth instant health or instantly dieth. In that stone the
bones of St. Machaldus are said to rest, yet nothing is found
therein save the clear water only; and though many have often-
times endeavoured to remove the stone, and especially the
King of the Norici (of Norway ?), who subdued the island, that
he might at all times have sweet water, yet have they all failed
in their attempts; for the deeper they dug to raise the stone, so
much the more deeply and firmly did they find it fixed in the
heart of the earth.

cognominata.   Habetur etiam in cœmeterio Ecclesiæ ejusdem
loci sarcophagus cavati lapidis, in quo latex jugiter resudat,
immo sufficienter scaturit, qui hausta dulcis, gustu salubris, mul-
tis infirmitatibus et præcipue veneno infectis, vel potatis, mederi
consuescit.   Aut enim post aquæ potationem qui libet celerem
sanitatem sentiet, aut cita morte vitam finiet.   In hoc etiam
Sancti Machaldi ossa sacra requievisse referuntur, in quo nihil,
nisi aqua limpida, invenitur.   Plures etiam pluries lapidem
illum a loco amovero et etiam Rex Noricorum ut aquam dulcem
haberet jugiter in mari, qui insulam subjugavit, conati sunt;
sed tamen affectu suo omnino frustrati sunt.   Quo etiam altius,
ut lapidem effoderent, nisi suffodere sunt, eo firmius et profun-
dius fixus inventus est in corde terræ.   (Sexta vita Patricii,
Trias. Thaum. p. 98, sec. clii.)

    Such is the legendary account of the most celebrated of the
bishops of the Manx church.   The history given of him by
Jocelinus, and reprinted by Colgan in the Fourth Life, is merely
an embellished edition of the version given in the Book of
Armagh.   To it we can only add in the words of Prudentius,
corruptela, dolus, commenta, insomnia, sordes.   Like his cele-

brated predecessor, St. Patrick, he is said to have attained to
a very advancèd period of life, and to have died at the age of
one hundred and ten years.

Although the above account of the years of St. Maughold is
not without exceptions, and must be received with caution, it
is only another instance, amongst the many we possess, of the
tendency of mediæval writers to deal in the marvellous, and
bestow upon their heroes a patriarchal age. Maughold's early
career, as we have just seen, is stated to have been one of
rapine and profligacy,—a mode of life little conducive to lon-
gevity. So if we concede, that by reason of his strength, the
number of his days may have been eighty, or even ninety
years, we shall in all probability have reached the limit of his
existence. Irish annalists, however, with singular unanimity,
state the year of Maughold's death to be 554,—a date which
makes his age at the time of dissolution, one hundred and ten
and upwards, supposing St. Patrick to have arrived in Ireland
between the years 440-444. At this epoch he could only have
been an infant,* and not the leader of a band of *kerns,* or free-
booters, as stated by his biographers. If, however, we grant that
Maughold was a predatory chieftain, as represented, and survived to the age of ninety, he must at all events have been
eighteen years old at the time of St. Patrick's advent; in which
case the remainder of his days would be seventy-two years, and
the date of obit 534 instead of 554, the truditionary period;†
a portion of time sufficiently great to enable him to devise and
carry out the ecclesiastical system I have ascribed to him.‡

---

* His festival day is the 25th of April. (Colgan's *Actt. SS.*)

† The date of his *floruit,* then, would be between the years 444 and 534.
The *Annals of Ulster* place his obit A.D. 488.

‡ According to the above view, Maughold was the first bishop, *de facto,* of
the Manx church, over which he presided for the long period of fifty-eight
years. With Stillingfleet and Lloyd, I have discarded Hector Boece's ridiculous bishop called *Amphibalus,* and consigned this absurdity to oblivion.
Maughold was consecrated by Conindrius and Romailus A.D. 455, eleven
years after his arrival in Man. Before him there could have been no bishop,

The history of the ancient church of Man, then, may be divided into two distinct and well-defined periods; the first of
which, comprising its[[earliest condition, extends from the fifth
to the commencement of the twelfth century; and the second,
from the foundation of Rushen Abbey, in 1134, to its decline
in the early part of the fourteenth. It is with the first of
these periods we have to do, as embracing the epoch which
gave rise to our cabbals, keeills, and treen churches, the
remains of which still so largely exist. These edifices are
chiefly interesting as being, in the absence of all historic record,
the only indices in existence of the state of Christianity in the
Isle of Man in the primitive ages. They carry us back to periods
that have bequeathed no written explanation of their origin,
though they show us how gradually, but completely, the influ-
ences of Christianity had spread over this island, in an age not
altogether barbaric, but of a civilisation different to our own.
Simple as these churches are, and devoid of architectural pre-
tensions, they are full of interest to the antiquary, and will be
so to him as long as civilisation endures. The existence of a
solitary tumulated ruin in a field, undisturbed for ages, merely
because it is called a " keeill," is a striking instance of the veneration with which the Manx people regard their sacred edifices; and to this feeling we owe the preservation of so many of
these interesting memorials of a bygone age.

TREEN LANDS.

The Isle of Man, as is well known, is divided into a number
of sections designated " Treen lands"; and these, again, into

for there was no church, as Conindrius and his coadjutor, Romailus, were
not diocesan, but missionary bishops, *episcopi vagantes*, who after they had
planted Christianity in the Isle of Man, returned to their own country.

* A treen is a manorial division of land. Each parish is divided into a
varying number of treens distinguished by different names. In 1505 the
treen rents, or *Reddita Tertiana*, meant division into thirds, and were consequently rents of the three Sheadings attached to each of the castles of Peel
and Rushen. The land contained in a treen is now wholly quarterland, but
formerly Intacks were included up to 1526. In 1706 they were taken from
the treens.

subsections called "Quarterlands,"—in Manx *kerroo valla*. Originally each treen contained a small place of worship styled "the treen church"; so that treen lands were, in fact, rudimentary parishes. This partition of the soil is of extremely ancient date, being coeval with the introduction of Christianity into the island. The meaning of the word "treen," as applied to these lands, has been the source of considerable discussion, though without throwing much light upon the subject. Some deduce it from the Manx word *strooan* (a stream), thought to indicate a portion of land between two streams,—a supposition not borne out by any fact. Another definition has been offered by the Rev. Wm. Mackenzie, who derives it from *jeih* (ten) and *raane* (a surety), arguing that each treen consisted of ten families, and each parish of ten treens. This explanation, which is merely a revival of the Saxon tything and hundred, makes the treens amount to one hundred and seventy,—a considerably greater number than exist. Nor was it the case that the quarterland owners, the union of whose estates constituted the treen lands, were in any way sureties or bondsmen either for themselves or for others. They were Odallers, whose right in the soil was absolute; and though they had certain duties to perform in connexion with the treen to which they belonged, they were voluntary, and for the general good.

The origin and meaning of the word, however, appears to be that pointed out by the Rev. J. G. Cumming,* as derived from the Manx word *tree* (three) and synonymous with *trian* in Irish and Gaelic, and *traian* or *traean* in Welsh. In the Manx language the word "treen" is defined to be "a township dividing tithe into three"; and in accordance with this definition is the fact that in Olave I's reign (A.D. 1134), the tithes† of the

* See the valuable notes to Sacheverell's account of the Isle of Man, edited for the Manx Society by the Rev. J. G. Cumming, M.A. P. 186.

† "Huic" (Bishop Reginald) "primo tertiæ ecclesiarum Manniæ a personis concessæ fuerunt ut deinceps liberi ab omni episcopali exactione fore potuissent." (*Chronicon Manniæ.*)

island were distributed in conformity with the above rendering
of the word,—one portion going to the bishop, another to the
Abbey of Rushen, and the remainder to the clergy.* Several
of our parishes still show that the principle of division by thirds
was the ancient practice adopted in this island. Ballaugh, for
instance, is divided into the *sea*, the *middle*, and the *fell* thirds,
—an arrangement evidently designed for the convenience of
the tithingman. In the application of thirds to treen lands,
however, as they at present stand, this principle does not
wholly apply ; for though we find a great many to˙ consist of
three quarterlands, there are some which contain only two,
others four, and some considerably higher ;† an irregularity I
believe to have been occasioned, in course of time, through alterations of boundaries, alienations, and sales of portions of
quarterlands. In the oldest account‡ we have of the Isle of
Man—a metrical history written in the commencement of the
sixteenth century—a treen is stated to consist of three estates
(*treen balley*) united for ecclesiastical purposes, and this probably was its ancient condition. Upon the *treen balley* devolved
the obligation of erecting and maintaining the treen church,
the formation of burial-grounds, and other duties now merged
in the parochial system. Each of these diminutive parishes
contained its own church, the service of which was conducted
either through the instrumentality of itinerant clerics, or else the
ministrations of one of the heads of the *treen balley*. At this

* It is remarkable in connection with the above distribution of the tithes,
that no provision seems to have been made for the maintenance of the poor.
(They were relieved by the monastic foundations, which had a third of the
tithes.)
    † Though the number of treens now existing amount to one hundred and
fifty, or thereabouts, there is reason to believe that originally they may not
have exceeded half this number ; as we find some treens, as Howstrake, for
instance, contain six quarterlands ; others ten ; and some, as the treen of
Commessary, Malew, twelve quarterlands to the treen. This great dissimila-
rity in size is explicable on the supposition, that anciently the treen was
larger than we find it at present ; or else that in process of time, two or
more became incorporated into one, and produced the present irregularity.
    ‡ A MS. ballad in the Rolls Office, styled *Mannanan Beg Mac y Leirr*.

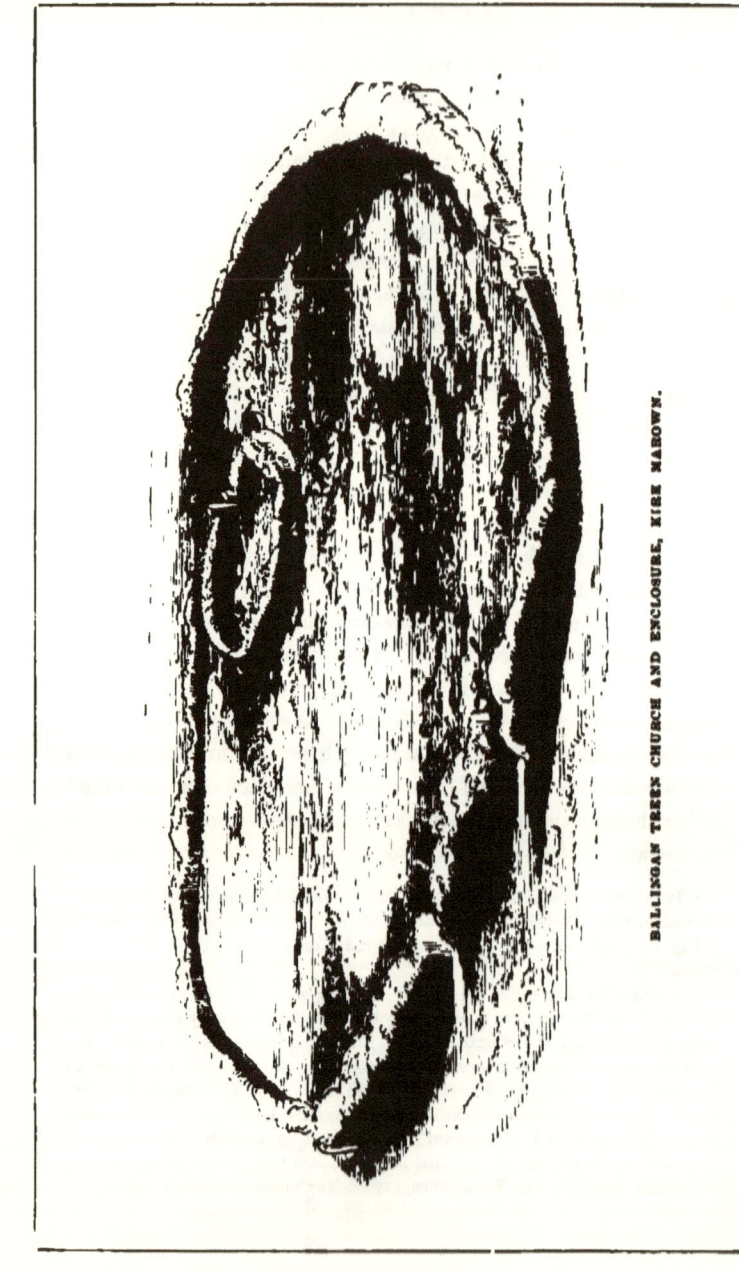

BALLINGAN TREEN CHURCH AND ENCLOSURE, KIRK MAROWN.

period the Manx church was purely diocesan ; there were no benefices, and the bishop was the sole incumbent, assisted by a few presbyters who lived with him, and were his assistants and council for the diocese at large. The system of treen lands and churches arose out of the exigencies of the times. Small chapels or churches of the rudest formation had sprung up everywhere, many isolated, and few, if any, canonically disciplined ; so that like the Irish churches of the same period, they required re-modeling. St. Maughold commenced the work ; and in the formation of the *treen balley,* we have probably one of the earliest attempts at a parochial system in Britain.

ECCLESIOLOGY.

It is to be regretted that the Isle of Man possesses no record of its ancient ecclesiastical edifices—not even a fragmentary notice that such a class of buildings as churches ever existed prior to the twelfth century ; and were it not for a passing allusion to the subject by Jocelinus, and the monks of Rushen Abbey, we should be, as far as history goes, absolutely churchless. Consequently the archæologist has nothing to assist him in his investigations, except tradition and his own researches. The difficulties in his way also are greatly increased through the extremely early epoch in which the Manx cabbals and keeills originated ; and from the circumstance, that few are now to be found in a tolerable state of preservation. Many present only the appearance of an old hedge, and others a shapeless mass of stones and earth, the combined results of decay, and the industry of the agriculturist, who utilises them as a convenient receptacle for the upturnings of the plough. A remarkable circumstance in connection with these cabbals and keeills, is the number that at one period must have existed, as some hundreds still remain.* Two orientations are also noticeable, one east and west, and the other towards the point

* The Ordnance Survey, at the present engaged in this island, seems to show, that anciently there was a chapel to every quarterland.

of the horizon where the sun rose on the saint's day to whom
the church was dedicated. In their materials and construction
they correspond with the account given in the *Book of Armagh* of similar places of worship in Ireland of the age of St.
Patrick. When the apostle visited Tirawley " he built there a
quadrangular church of moist earth, because there was no wood
near."* Here we have an exact description of the Manx cabbal,
and there can be no doubt that the primitive churches of Ireland formed the model of the Manx. It is singular that amongst
the numerous remains of these churches scattered throughout
the island, there is not an instance to be found of any built in
the crucial, semi-circular, or octagonal forms ; nor is there an
example of cyclopean architecture in the Isle of Man, although
an approach to it may be occasionally noticed. The result is,
the style is in every instance alike, one embracing the utmost
simplicity and uniformity of design. Consequently the cabbal
and keeill are invariably quadrangular; the lights oblong, or
quadrilateral openings splaying inwards, and the stonework of
the doors and windows unchiselled. This uniformity of design
no doubt had its origin in the veneration felt for some ancient
model given to the people by their first teachers, independent
of any abstract considerations arising out of primitive causes.
Hence we find their archaic form, slightly altered, still preserved
in our parish churches, as may be seen in the rectangular shape,
absence of chancel and couched semi-circular absis. In few of
them moreover do we find any traces of an altar. If they
contained any, they were simply *altataria portatilia*, or domestic altars, removable at pleasure.

It is singular, in connection with the history of the Manx
church, that there is hardly a record of sacred relics having been
introduced into the Isle of Man.† There are no examples of

* " Fecit ibi ecclesiam terrenam de humo quadratam quia non prope erat
silva." (Terecham, *Lib. Armac.*, fol., 1466.)

† There were the " three relics of Man" ordered to be borne before the
Lord in the great Tynwald days. See vol. iii *Manx Society*, page 72 ; and in
a roll of 32 Henry VIII (1541) mention is made of "one hand and one
Bysshope hede," which were probably reliquaries.

The Mena Cabbal of the Fifth Century.

saints leading an eremitic life. It is difficult to account
for this, unless on the supposition that such incentives to
religious devotion were held to be valueless, and consequently
rejected. At this epoch, the Manx church seems to have
approximated more closely to the first churches of Asia,
than at any subsequent date. The worship was simple and
unadorned, and the bishops elected by the unanimous voices
of the clergy and laity, and not, as in modern times, by a *congé
d'élire* from the crown. Neither did the people pay tithes, but
supported their pastors by voluntary oblations, which in these
days were probably sufficient for the purpose, as we find no
mention made of other sources of revenue, such as obventions,
altarage, and mortuary dues. From this we learn that the
church was deambulatory, and had neither cathedral, dean, nor
chapter.

The foregoing are the chief features of Manx churches, prior
to the middle ages. I shall now describe them in detail, according to the following classification :—

THE CABBAL.

THE KEEILL.

THE TREEN CHURCH.

THE MORTUARY CHAPEL, AND BURIAL GROUND.

THE CABBAL.

The Isle of Man, unlike England or Ireland, never possessed
any churches built either of wattles or wood. The reason of
this was the scarcity of timber; whilst, on the other hand,
stones and sods were abundant, and offered an unlimited supply
of a more durable material. I have mentioned that the churches
of the fifth century were called "Cabbals," and I shall confine
myself in this section to a description of these edifices, as the
oldest places of worship in the island, and the original form of
building in which the Gospel was first preached to the Manx
people.

The cabbal is an earthen structure, quadrangular in form,

G

of very small dimensions, and rarely exceeds twelve feet in length, by nine in breadth. It is invariably situated on a low truncated hillock of artificial formation, called the "chapel mound," and enclosed by a sod fence. There is no burial place attached to it, as the Manx did not in the fifth century inter in consecrated ground. Up to the ninth century, we find the same plan still adhered to in the elevation of the church and churchyard above the level of the adjacent land; the design is evidently the embodying of the scriptural principle, of a church set upon a hill being a visibly conspicuous object. In the early examples, the plateola within the vallum is of very small dimensions, scarcely allowing sufficient room for three persons abreast to pass between the chapel and the circumvallation. The walls of the cabbal are low, pyramidal in form, and of great width at base. They never exceed five feet in height, and are constructed to carry a low-pitched sod or heather roof. (See plate, "Manx Cabbal of the fifth century.") In the inside they measure from a foot to a foot and a half more than externally, in consequence of the floor being sunk to that extent to heighten the interior. The entrance to these chapels is through a small opening in the south-west angle of the gable. This doorway, in the greater part of the cabbals of the fifth century, had neither jambs nor lintels, and was also the only source of light to the interior. To protect the inside from effects of the weather, the contrivance made use of was a bundle of gorse, or a screen of faggots laid across the doorway, and called in the Manx language, *skeiy sy doarlish,* "a bundle of faggots in a gap."

The mode of construction of the cabbal was as follows:— A suitable spot having been selected, the builders threw up a small conical truncate mound from three to four feet high, and around the edge of the truncated portion built a low sod wall. Within the enclosed space the cabbal was erected, not in the centre of the plateola, but towards its eastern portion, and formed of the same materials as the circumvallation. In these churches there were no seats, the congregation standing during

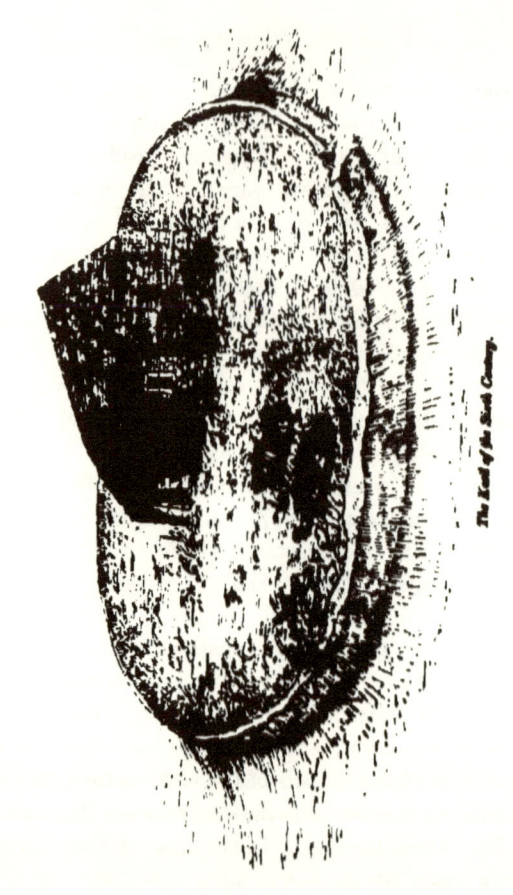

The Mask of the Sixth Century.

divine worship, so that the service would necessarily be of short duration, and most likely wholly consisted in the adorations of prayer and praise.

THE KEEILL.

In the preceding section I have described the cabbal as it existed in the fifth century, and now come to a better class of buildings denominated Keeills, introduced about the middle of the sixth. These churches are of two kinds : one built wholly of stone, and the other of a mixture of sods and stones. They are larger than the cabbals, and measure from fifteen to twenty foot in length by twelve in breadth, but rarely exceed these dimensions. Both have burial grounds within the circumvallation ; but

A.

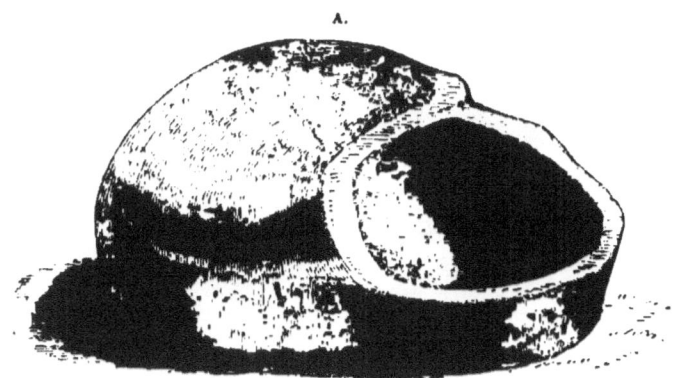

Stone Font, Keeill Pharic, Ballafieer Kirk. Marown.

through the absence of all external indications of the nature of the place, most observers would pass it by unnoticed. In a few instances the keeill carries a slate roof. It has also side lights, and a door of entrance in the south wall. (See plate.) Rude stone vessels called " fonts " are sometimes found within them, and occasionally a quadrangular recess is observed in the east wall. Like the cabbal, the keeill also stands upon artificially raised ground, is rectangular in form, and altogether better built than

G 2

the former. In the superior examples, the interstices of the masonry are filled up with mould, to steady the stone work and exclude the weather. The mode of construction of the keeill was similar to the cabbal. The following account given by Bede of the building of St. Cuthbert's Church, Lindisfarn, in 684, so exactly describes the method pursued in the Isle of Man, that I quote it in preference to giving another :—

" The church was round, and about four or five perches wide between the walls. On the outside the wall was the height of a man ; in the inside higher, so made by sinking a huge rock, done to prevent the thoughts from rambling, by restraining the sight. The walls were neither of squared stone, nor brick, nor cemented with mortar, but of rough unpolished stone, with

B.

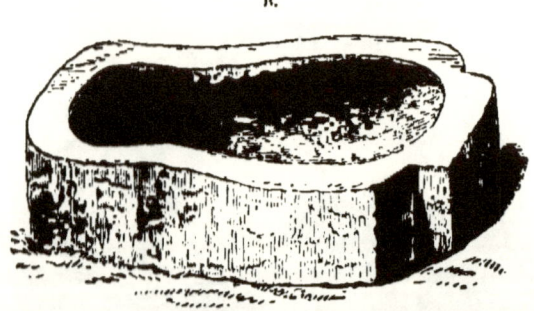

Stone Font, St. Lingan's, Kirk Marown.

turf dug up in the middle of the place and banked on both sides all round. Some of the stones were so big that four men could scarcely lift one. The roof was constructed of unhewn timber and thatched."*

The annexed view of the ruins of St. Lingan's Treen Keeill and enclosure, Marown, will give the reader a correct idea of one of these old places of worship. It is situated on the Ballingan estate adjoining Ballaguinney, about a mile and a

* Beda Vit. Cudberti, p. 243.

DOORWAY, BALLAQUINNEY TREEN CHAPEL.

quarter from the Peel Road, and is one of the best specimens
existing of our insular keeills. The enclosure in which stands
the keeill is one hundred and eight feet long by sixty-three
feet broad, ovicular in form, and in an excellent state of preservation. This is the necropolis of the church. In the south-
east part lies St. Lingan's. The portion of the walls remaining measure four feet high by three feet thick, but the masonry
is of a much superior description than is usual in keeills of the
sod and stone formation. In the west end there has once been
a window, but it is now entirely destroyed by visitors using it
as a short cut into the church. The doorway is in the south-
east angle, and guarded by two inclining monolithic jambs
supported by rubble stonework, so regular as to have the
appearance of ashlar masonry. (See plate.)

Doorway, Keeill, St. Lingan, Marown.

In the north-east angle of the church, deeply embedded in
the ground, lies the font. (See plate B, p. 84.) It measures
one foot eleven inches long, by ten and a half inches broad.
The interior walling of the west end is concave, and gives it
the appearance of a couched semi-circular absis. It is, how-

ever, nothing more than irregular masonry producing this
effect. The gentleman* who owns the property, with a laud-
able motive, has planted the enclosure with trees to protect it
from injury. An example we should wish to see more followed.

Interior Walling of Ballaquinney Treen Keeill, Marown.

Though I have stated that stone churches were not in use in
the Isle of Man till the close of the sixth century, there was
one exception to the contrary as early as the fifth. This was
the church built by St. Maughold on the headland near Ramsey
bearing his name. Although I have characterised it as a church,
it was a conventual establishment, partaking of the Irish type
of that period, and consisted of the church, the bishop's residence, and cells for ecclesiastical and other purposes, enclosed
by a double embankment of unusual strength. The existing
plateau contains three acres of ground, and originally must
have been much larger, as only a segment of it now remains,
having the shape of the letter R. It differed from its Irish
archetypes in being surrounded by a double circumvallation,
and in having the cemetery within the enclosure. From the
strength and height of the embankments, they seem to have
been intended for defensive purposes, and are probably a later

* J. J. Carran, Esq.

The Truro Church of the Eighth Century.

addition to the churchyard, the work of the Pagan Norsemen
when in possession of this Isle.* It is not impossible, however, that they may have been erected by St. Maughold himself or his immediate successors; for, at the period when he
built his church, before heathenism was fully eradicated, and
whilst the Manx people were still in a perturbed and instable
state, it is probable that latent feelings of hostility to the new
faith remained, which rendered the adoption of precautionary
measures a matter of necessity. However this may be, it was
from this spot, the school of learning and the centre of civilisation in the Isle of Man, that issued that noble band of eccle-
siastics who finally established the Christian faith, and left
behind them in the crumbling walls of the cabbal and keeill
memorials of their pious labours that have long survived the
memory of those who reared them.

THE TREEN CHURCH.

We now come to an entirely different class of buildings, in-
termediate between the keeills and the churches of the middle
ages. These are the true *treen* churches, introduced towards
the close of the eighth century. They differ from their predecessors in form and construction, and in presenting a more
regular style of architecture. The masonry is still rude, but

* Since the above was written this view has to some extent been confirmed
by recent discoveries in the churchyard. Within the last few weeks a portion of the southern extremity of the inner embankment has been removed,
in consequence of alterations making in the cemetery. Beneath it a substantial stone wall has been exhumed, and close to it a heap of ashes. These
consist of charcoal, bone ashes, and minute globules of lead. The Rev. Wm.
Stainton Moses, to whom I am indebted for the above information, suggests,
that the wall may be a portion of the ancient boundary of the churchyard,
and probably runs the entire length of the vallum. As this can only be determined by an examination of the whole structure, it must remain for future
investigation. The ashes, however, show, that at one period, heathen rites
have been celebrated here; and these must have been either anterior to the
introduction of Christianity, or else subsequent to that event. In the latter
case, they can only be ascribed to the Pagan Norsemen, during their occupancy of this island.

for the first time we find it put together with cement.* The entrances now carry doors suspended from inclining monolithic jambs. The side lights are more numerous, and a rudimentary bell turret surmounts the western gable. In dimensions these churches do not exceed the keeills, averaging from fifteen to twenty feet long, by ten in breadth. The roofs are high pitched, and the general appearance more imposing than their predecessors. A remarkable alteration is now noticeable. The chapel mound and raised graveyard have disappeared, and the whole partakes more of the characteristics of churches of modern times. They appear to be the originals from which those of the present day have been modelled.

The following description of the Treen of Ballakilley, Malew (see plate), lying three miles north-east of the parish church, will enable the reader to form some idea of the architectural arrangements of these edifices. The treen is situated about fifty yards from the farm house. Its dimensions inside are twenty-one feet long, by nine in breadth. The western gable, crowned with ivy, is still standing, but the east end is in ruins, and blocked to the height of the remaining portion by quantities of fallen masonry. This church has a very peculiar appearance from the walls being built of rounded boulders of granite and quartz, giving to the whole the resemblance of a pile of cannon balls. Their height is six feet three inches from the ground to the spring of the roof; and the western gable sixteen feet nine inches to the peak. In the south wall near the eastern angle is the door of entrance, five feet two inches in height, by two feet six inches at base, and diminishing upwards to two feet. Opposite it, in the north side, is a square headed window, and another in the south wall near the west end. This window externally is two feet six inches high, by

---

* The cement made use of is a tenacious plastic clay, which in time hardens almost to stone. Lime mortar was not known in the Isle of Man till the middle of the tenth century, and was first employed in the building of Castle Rushen.

ono foot six inches broad splaying inwards. Internally it measures two feet six inches high, by three feet broad. In the north-west angle of the gable is a similar window, measuring one foot five inches long, by nine inches broad, and splaying internally to one foot five inches in length, by one foot eight inches in breadth, so that the external and internal measurements are reversed. The cemetery has long been under cultivation, and cannot now bo distinguished, but it yearly discloses before the plough of the husbandman numerous remnants of mortality.

The Mortuary Chapel.

The chief of the mortuary chapels now remaining in the Isle of Man is St. Luke's, a small edifice in ruins, lying on the western slope of the *Cronk-na-Irey Lhaa,* in the parish of Kirk Christ Rushen. It is traditionally known as the church and cemetery of the Danish kings. The neighbouring village of Dalby, two miles west of the chapel, was anciently a Scandinavian settlement, supposed to have been founded by an offset from the Danish conquerors of England, who gave to the place a celebrity and a name. Be this as it may, the present insignificant village shows no indications now of ever having been a place of importance, much less an abode of royalty. From it the funeral processions embarked for St. Luke's (? St. Leoc's), and landed at the foot of the ravine, between the *Cronk-na-Irey-Lhaa* and the *Carnanes.* This is the most feasible way of reaching the mountain from Dalby, as the approach to it by land is both difficult and dangerous.* Beneath the chapel on the beach is the Fern cave, abounding in almost every variety of this admired plant. Nothing can exceed its beauty. From the roof and walls hang, in graceful festoons, thousands of ferns of the most

* The best way of reaching the chapel is by means of a boat from Fleswick Bay, and sailing thence round the headland of *Ennyn Mooar.* A little further on is a small rocky point running into the sea from the Carnanes. This is the entrance to the ravine leading to the church and cemetery.

brilliant emerald hue; and when the setting sun illumines the cavern, it lights up the place with rays of gold with magic effect.

St. Luke's, styled in a bull of Pope Eugenius III the monastery of St. Leoc, is simply a mortuary chapel, erected for the offices of the dead. It is built upon a spur of the mountain, about one hundred and fifty yards from the edge of a steep precipice. A portion of its walls only remain, and these in summer are so overgrown with fern as to be entirely hidden from view. The cemetery lies on the north side, and is a very picturesque object. It is bisected in its longitudinal diameter by a pathway fringed with boulder quartz of dazzling whiteness. From the end of this walk, a branch diverges to the south in a zig-zag manner, but originally it was prolonged northwards as well, and so formed the western boundary of the cemetery. This pathway terminates in the outer enclosure of the chapel. (See plate.)

St. Luke's, like the koeills, is a stone erection built without cement of any kind, but the masonry is more regular, and much better constructed than in the case of the latter. The floor, paved with pebbly stones, can with difficulty be seen, from the mass of debris encumbering the place. The chapel in its perfect state must have been of very diminutive size, and could scarcely have exceeded eight feet in height to the peak of the roof, as its interior only measures eleven feet by nine. St. Luke's differs from all similar places in the island, in having a double circumvallation encompassing it for two-thirds of the plateau. In the lower or western portion of the outer circle, are indications of its having been used as a place of sepulture, but the mode of inhumation has not yet been investigated. In the inner circle stands the chapel, from which a pathway leads between two stone pillars to the ravine. This glen, studded with masses of white quartz, has a very beautiful effect, and will amply repay the tourist for the trouble of visiting it. Such are the chief features of the chapel and burial ground of the Danish kings. With a brief notice of the mode of inhumation

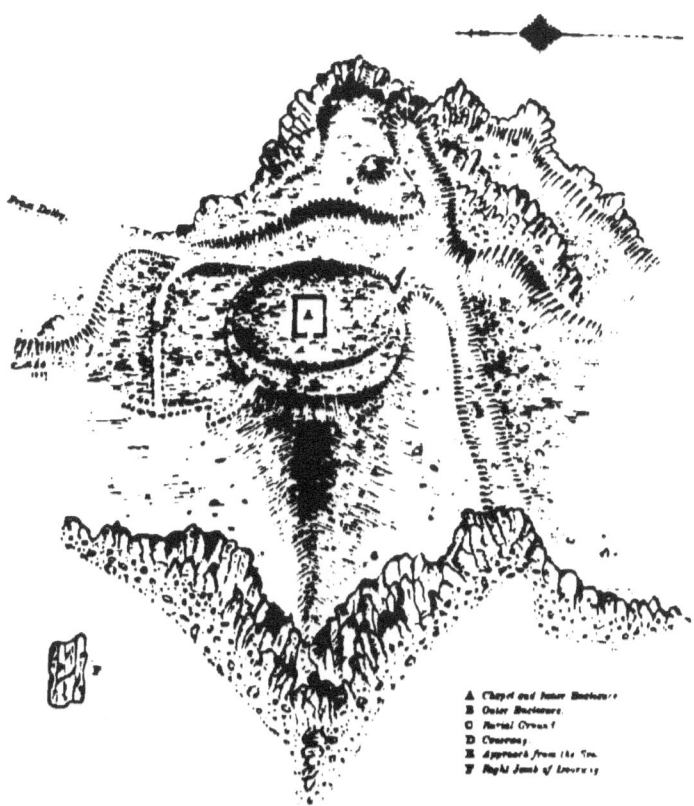

A   Chapel and Inner Enclosure
B   Outer Enclosure.
C   Burial Ground.
D   Causeway.
E   Approach from the Sea.
F   Right Jamb of Doorway.

St. Luke's Chapel, and Burial Ground of the Danish Kings.
Cronk-na-Irey-Lhaa.

practised in these cemeteries, I shall conclude this account of Manx churches prior to the middle ages.

The burial of the dead in the Isle of Man was essentially a religious belief, involving a lively faith in the resurrection, consequently the selection of a burial place, the *ubi resurgere*, where the dead might rest in peace to rise again in glory, was an object of the utmost importance. Hence these cemeteries usually occupy picturesque and retired localities, with little to awake the sympathy of the casual visitor, except the sanctity of the place. They contain no monumental stones, or other memorials of the dead, to indicate who rests below, but great and small lie mingled together without distinction in the one common hope of a joyful resurrection.

The mode of inhumation practised was as follows:—A grave three feet deep and two feet wide was dug east and west, and lined with flag-stones to the height of fifteen inches. In it the corpse was laid wrapt in a mort-cloth, and closed in by a coverlid of stones. (See Keeill of sixth century, opposite page 83.) A few shovelsful of earth and a layer of sods completed the remainder. No implements or relics of any kind were entombed along with it, but the whole betokens the simple burial of the early Christian church.

It sometimes happens that two, and even three bodies, rest in the same grave. When this is the case, they will be found to lie on their sides with the lower extremities semi-flexed. In consequence of this, the stone coffin is much smaller in size than is usually the case, and has more the appearance of a child's than an adult's burial. Very seldom the remains contained in these graves will bear handling, unless the surrounding soil happen to be of a dry and sandy nature. Their colour is generally of a rusty iron, or tan hue, caused by the quantity of ferruginous matter contained in the schistose formations of this island. The crania belong to the dolichocephalic type.

Burials in stone-lined graves continued in use in the Isle of Man down to a comparatively recent date, and did not finally cease until the commencement of the seventeenth century.

VII.

NOTES ON THE STONE MONUMENTS IN THE ISLE OF MAN.

BY THE REV. E. L. BARNWELL.

IF the stone monuments in the Isle of Man are not remarkable for their dimensions or their state of preservation, they have at least an interest wanting in similar remains in Wales, Cornwall, or other districts where these monuments are not uncommon. Generally speaking, such monuments are supposed to be, and probably are, the relics of a certain race, or divisions of it, whether Celtic or of an earlier unknown people. They may and seem to have been erected at different periods; but they were still erected by the same race, or by its successive waves. The case of the Isle of Man is different. Within the historic period it has been overrun by Norsemen, themselves builders of structures of a similar character, although presenting certain distinct features of their own. Had their monuments, then, as well as the earlier ones of their predecessors, been left in any moderate state of preservation, the assignment of each class to their respective builders would have been in most cases comparatively easy; but in their present condition of almost complete destruction, the attempt to distinguish one from the other with certainty is almost hopeless. To add to the difficulty, few satisfactory accounts of the contents of graves opened in later times, and no trustworthy delineations of the monuments themselves, before their destruction, have come down to us. It is true that the work of rifling and destruction, especially of the earliest examples, may have taken place centuries ago, even by the Scandinavian invaders themselves, in their search for gold and other treasure.   On the Continent, as in the north-western districts of France, the Northmen appear to have ransacked every grave that promised such booty ; but in many instances they have left behind them, as of little value, articles of great importance to the archæologist of the present day.   If the same spoliation was practised by the Scandinavians in Man, they carried on the work so effectually as to leave little hopes to the Manx explorer.   There may, however, still remain, especially in less frequented parts of the island, graves which may have wholly or partially escaped ; and if such should be the case, it is to be earnestly hoped that they will be carefully examined by gentlemen competent to superintend the operations ; for the safest, if not the only reliable means of ascertaining any real information respecting the habits and uses of the earlier races, which once occupied the island, can be obtained in no other manner than by a careful examination of such relics.

There are, however, certain distinctive features exhibited in the various remains throughout Man which deserve attention. The late Dr. Oswald has, indeed, in his *Vestigia*, chapter ii, given a full and accurate description of the most remarkable ; but his deductions and observations, especially as regards Druidic theories, must be received with great caution.   Besides his indiscriminate use of the term " Druidic circle," and "altar," he introduces us to a distinction between the complete circle and the semi-lunar forms, which, he says, have been supposed to have been respectively dedicated to the sun and moon.   In the days of Stukely such theories may have been suggested, but would hardly be advanced in the middle of the present century, and certainly should not have been repeated without some explanatory caution by so good and zealous an archæologist as the author of the *Vestigia*; for although it is now universally agreed among the most competent judges, that these various circles are simply portions of sepulchral arrangements, yet there is even at the present day a certain class who see in them nothing but Bardic and Druidic mysteries. Thus these semi-lunar forms are said to be connected with lunar worship,— the circle with that of the sun ; whereas the former are but mutilated remains of the latter, whilst these latter are but the relics of a grave.

In the present notice, stone monuments will alone be touched on. The numerous early earthworks, of different forms and intended for various purposes, scattered through the island, form a class by themselves well deserving a separate examination, although a good account of many of them will be found in the *Vestigia*, and is given in the previous Memoir by Dr. Oliver.

Of the cromlech proper there does not appear to be any example in the Isle of Man,—at least none such was seen during the meeting of the Association. Whether the small chamber in the Oatland circle is one, will be best decided by the spade, as without it it is not easy to determine whether the stones composing the sides of it were originally placed *on*, and not *within*, the ground ; for this seems to be the safest test to distinguish the one class from the other. According to this view, the cromlech is always built *on* the ground, the kistvaen sunk *within* it, so as in fact to become an ordinary rude stone coffin. A large kistvaen must not, therefore, be considered a small cromlech, as is sometimes the case. Thus the latter name has been given to the stone grave near Tynwald Mount, which has been laid bare by a cutting in the road.

It may be a question whether cromlechs are always of much older dates than the kistvaen, although the latter continued in use to a period when even the very nature and object of the cromlech had become a mystery. In the island especially it is difficult to say when the practice of burying in kistvaens ceased, as those opened at Cronk ny Keeillane and elsewhere are apparently Christian. The form, however, of such a grave is so simple and natural, that it is difficult to conceive that it is merely a kind of copy of the cromlech, or even much later. The two kinds of chambers were probably contemporaneous; the larger and more costly cromlech, with its covering tumulus, being only adopted for persons of distinction; for when we consider the enormous amount of labour that must have been spent in raising the covering stones, sometimes thirty feet long, and almost always of enormous thickness, on the top of supporters projecting six or more feet from the surface of the ground, and the additional labour of covering the whole with a huge mound of earth or stones, and how much of this

Rock at Ballamona.

toil might have been saved by merely sinking the slabs within the ground, it is evident that such a costly practice owes its origin to some tradition of the remotest antiquity, which may, perhaps, be traced in the rock-caves of the East, or even the Pyramids themselves, which look very much like simple tumuli over the remains of the dead. At Autun, in France, is the well-known mass of masonry, now robbed indeed of its ashlar, but which is simply a solid stone tumulus (if such a phrase is

admissible). These considerations point to the extreme antiquity of such monuments, usually ascribed to Celtic races,
but which may, and probably have been erected by some anterior people. But even allowing the great antiquity of the
cromlech proper, it by no means follows that the kistvaen was
unknown at the same early period.

Of the existing remains, however, in the island, which are
connected with sepulture, the large stone circles, more or less
perfect, may be placed among the earliest; although, in some
cases, it seems impossible to distinguish those which were
erected in later times by the Scandinavians. The large masses
of white quartz, mostly isolated or not arranged in any order,
seem to belong to the earlier class. A faithful representation
is given of one of them at p. 95. It lies on the land of Ballamona. Other similar masses in the same spot have been either
removed or completely destroyed, so that it is not possible to
ascertain in what order they were once grouped, for although
some may think that they have been brought to their present
situation by natural agency, yet the finding of several near one
another in a particular spot, where they do not naturally occur,
seems to indicate that they have been brought thither, and
that too at no little cost of labour. The hill above Malew
church, still retains two or three similar masses of white quartz,
which the author of the *Vestigia* seems to describe as having
formed a circle of about ten yards in diameter, although no
traces of it are now to be detected. He speaks of two of the
stones as portal stones, and of a third within the area, which
of course must be the altar stone in the eyes of those, who still
consider these circles connected with Druidic or Bardic mysteries, but which is more likely to be merely one of the stones
of the circle out of place.

As, however, the late Dr. Oswald seemed satisfied that such a
circle of quartz rocks did exist at Malew, it renders the conjecture probable that those at Ballamona also were portions of a
similar circle. It is also remarkable that the ground, which

PLAN OF OATLANDS CIRCLE, ISLE OF MAN.

A. Chamber B.
B. Stone with cup markings.
C. Stone, five feet high.
D. Stone, four feet six inches high.

E. Fallen stone—perhaps portion of
the covering stone.
F, G, H. Detached stones of outer
circle.

Average height of other stones of inner circle, three feet.

OATLANDS CIRCLE, ISLE OF MAN.

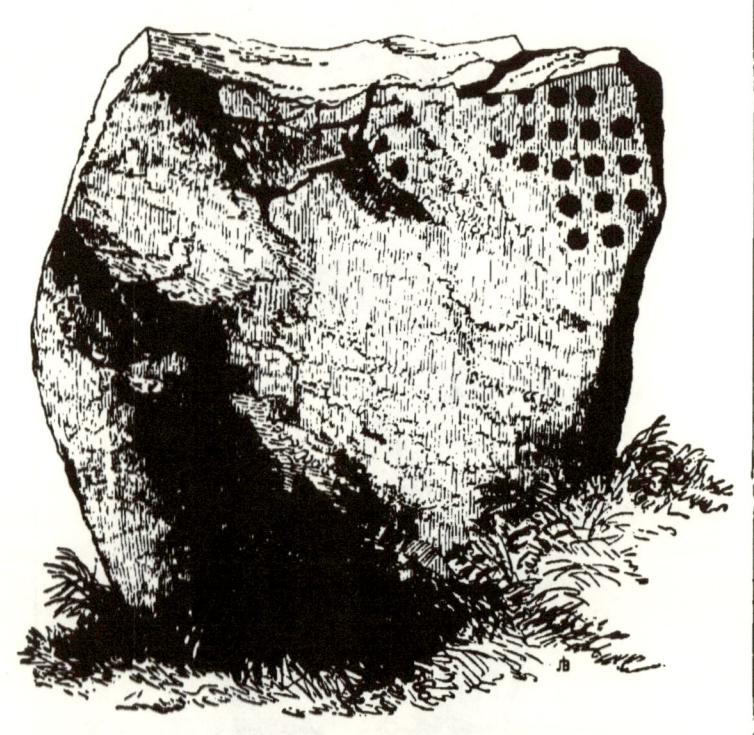

STONE, WITH CUP MARKINGS, OATLANDS CIRCLE, ISLE OF MAN.

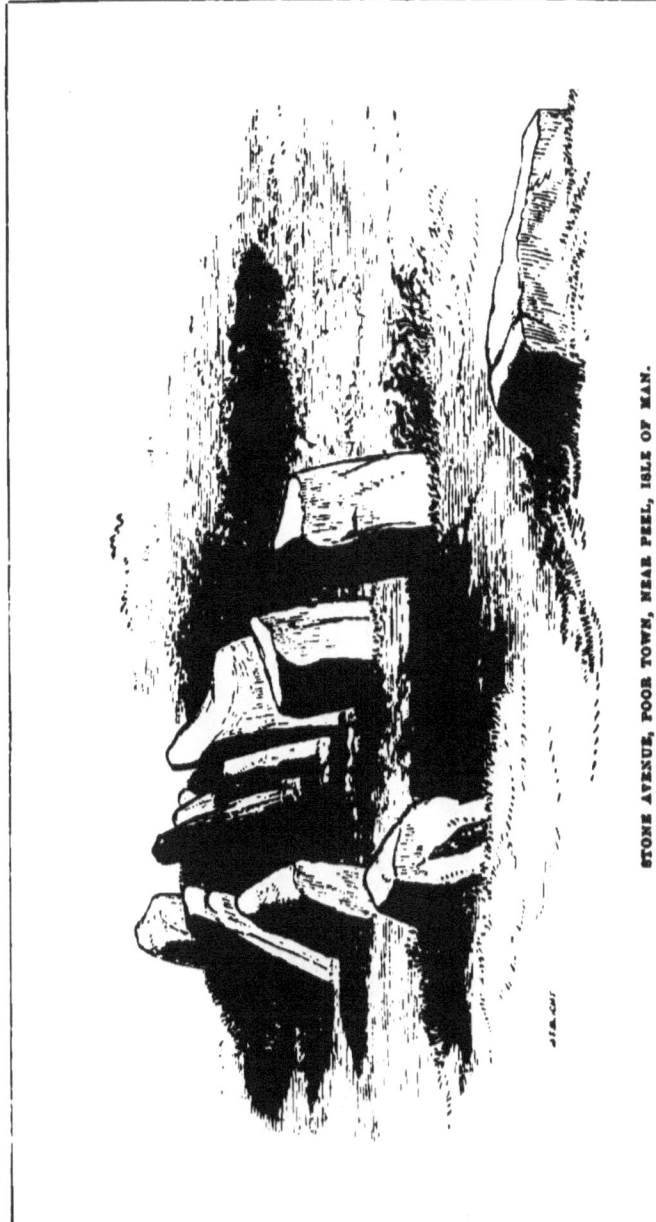

STONE AVENUE, POOR TOWN, NEAR PEEL, ISLE OF MAN.

CIRCLE ON THE MULL, ISLE OF MAN.

KISTVAEN, NEAR ST. JOHN'S TYNWALD MOUNT.

this circle may have occupied, has been an extensive cemetery. In addition to the neighbouring tumulus marking a grave, numerous kistvaens have from time to time been discovered in ploughing, the fragments of one of which, destroyed a short time ago, consisted of thin, slaty stones. A Treen chapel also is said to have stood on this spot, so that if it be a fact that a primitive stone circle of quartz masses also existed here, we have a remarkable instance of the same burial-ground having been used by various races down to Christian times.

The earth was excavated to a slight extent under the Balla-mona block, but nothing was discovered except the two small stones given in the cut, which appear at first sight to have been supporters to the mass, but which, from their diminutive size and their position, are suspiciously natural. A small fragment of vegetable charcoal was also found, but its presence, unsupported by other indications of fire, is not of much importance. If any traces of interment exist, they are likely to be found *near*, not *under* the quartz mass, as Mr. John Stuart has frequently found to be the case in Scotland during his numerous diggings in and about circles.

An important group of circles, known as the Mount Murray Circles, may be of a later period than those formed of quartz blocks. These circles are so imbedded in the heath that they are somewhat difficult to trace, although they are unusually perfect. If the ground could be cleared, it is not unlikely that traces of the once existing chambers might be made out. An upright stone in one of them has certain marks, which at first sight might be taken for artificial, but which do not appear to be so. This grouping of circles, almost, if not quite, in contact with each other, is not unusual, and seems to indicate an early character. In many instances, such groups have been included in one large circle, which sometimes remains when the enclosed circles and graves have vanished. Hence may be explained the mystery of circles like that near Penrith, known as Long Meg

and her daughters, which is evidently too large to have been
intended to surround a single grave.

The circles in Arragon also attracted attention, from the fact
that one of them had an inner circle of stones placed, not close
to the base of the tumulus, but some little distance up its sides.
This peculiarity was not observed in a circle in the next enclosure. This position of the stones indicates the Scandinavian
character of the tumulus.

Another tolerably perfect circle, composed of quartz blocks,
was pointed out by the Bishop of Sodor and Man. It is
situated not far from Bishop's Court, on high ground commanding a fine sea view. It is probably one of the earlier
class. The tumulus, which once existed, appears to have been
formed of fine soil, if that which still covers one of the stones,
as it seems to be, is a last remnant. If so, the soil must have
been too valuable to the farmer to have escaped removal. In a
small island like that of Man, no part of it can be called distant
from the sea; but the majority of this class of antiquities seem
to show that, when possible, the builders of them selected sites
commanding a sea view. In no instance is this tendency more
strongly exhibited than in Brittany, where, almost without exception, the great monuments are on the coast. The same may
be said of Wales in a less degree. Instances, no doubt, occur
where they are found more inland; but, as a general rule, the
earliest vestiges of man are to be found along the coast.

All the circles mentioned have lost the interior structure.
That at Oatlands is an exception, which retains its central
chamber. The inner circle of stones, placed near one another,
marks the limit of the carn or tumulus. Three stones of the
outer circle, placed at greater intervals, still remain.

The chamber itself is composed of substantial slabs of stone,
nor less substantial was the covering stone lying on the ground.
At present the chamber has the appearance of a kistvaen, but
it would be necessary to clear away the soil to ascertain whether
the sides were originally placed on the ground, in which case

it would be a small cromlech. But the most remarkable circumstance connected with it, is that one of the stones has several rows of the curious cups, to which Professor Simpson has called the attention of his brother-archæologists, and which until first noticed by that keen observer, seem to have been unknown, or at least to have never attracted attention. Now these cups, and their developments in the form of circles, are found only in the earlier class of stone monuments, so that there can be little hesitation in assigning the Oatlands group to the earliest period. The character of this monument, the cups, and whole arrangement, will be best understood from the accurate drawings and measurements taken on the spot by Mr. Blight, which are given in the accompanying illustrations. The cups are, however, shown more distinctly than they appear in the original.

There is a singular group of upright stones at Poortown on the old Peel road, forming a gallery. This gallery, covered with flat stones, was, together with the chamber to which it led, once covered with soil. In the great majority of existing cromlechs, all traces of a gallery conducting to the chamber have long since vanished, but in this instance the chamber has been destroyed, and the gallery left. It is, however, by no means certain that galleries always formed a portion of such structures; examples might be given where it is proved they never existed. One of the best authorities on this subject has suggested that the more important chambers were built with a view to subsequent interments, so that it would be necessary to have such a means of access without disturbing the tumulus or chamber; but that where this motive did not operate, the chamber was closed up, and no gallery added. The traces of such galleries are very rare in these islands. One, or rather the remains of one, exists in the cromlech on the Henblas estate in Anglesey, which was visited by the Cambrian Archæological Association during the Bangor Meeting. They are, however, common enough in Brittany.

If, however, the moderate height of these stones seems to
show that they could not have served as the walls of a gallery,
it is not impossible but that in this group we may have an example of the stone avenue or alignment ;—an arrangement
common enough in Brittany, but in these islands of the highest
rarity. The stones are, however, placed much nearer to each
other than is usual in an ordinary avenue, so that on the whole
it seems more probable that it is the remains of a covered
gallery to a grave. Under either supposition, however, it is
certainly one of the most interesting, if not *the* most interesting, of Manx stone monuments, and deserves to be carefully
protected from the destroyer.

This Manx example is composed of such small stones, that
unless the ground has been raised by natural causes, access
could not have been obtained in an upright position. But
this question can be determined by clearing away the soil,
which Mr. Harrison, the owner of the estate, has promised to
do. If there has been any accumulation of soil, the floor may
possibly remain, which is frequently formed of one or more of
large flags. Several large stones, which seem to have belonged
to this group, are now on the other side of the bank.

The stone monuments hitherto noticed are, with the exception
of the Arragon circles, most probably of the earlier kind. The
remarkable circle of graves on the hill above Port Erin may
belong to the same class, although they are not built of the
same substantial slabs, which generally characterise the earlier
chambers. Their remarkable grouping, however, so as to
form a perfect circle, and the fact of a small raised bank en-
closing the circle, seem to indicate a very early character.
There appears to have been more than one entrance into the
circle, although this appearance may have arisen from the dis-
placing of some of the stones. A reference, however, to the
ground plan, made by Mr. W. Matthews of the Government
Harbour works, will best show this peculiarity. There was not
sufficient time on the occasion of the visit to examine with

greater care these outlying stones, so as to ascertain whether they are original portions of the group. The general view is from a drawing made for the Association by Mr. Jeffcott of Castletown, who has, in a subsequent memoir, furnished some details concerning it. It is situated in the highest parts of the mountain called " The Mull," in the parish of Rushen, close to a rocky valley which gives to the monument its name, Rhullick-y-lagg

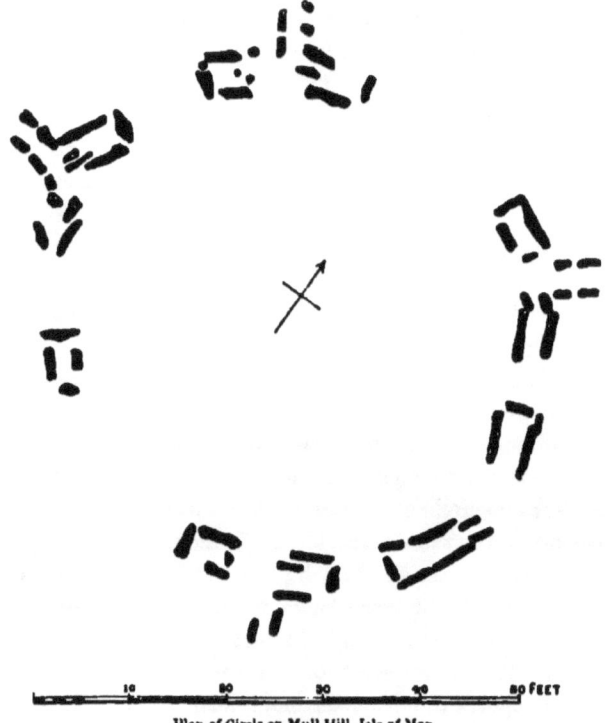

Plan of Circle on Mull Hill, Isle of Man.

Shliggagh, or " the grave-yard of the valley of broken slates." It was with no little difficulty that Mr. Jeffcott ascertained its Manx name, which, but for the information he obtained from two octogenarian natives, might have been entirely lost. The

materials of the kists have been evidently taken from the spot,
and vary much in thickness, namely from six to sixteen inches,
and are entirely without any marks of tooling. The interior
diameter of the circle is forty-six feet. It is very remarkable
that this curious circle had not hitherto attracted any attention,
or even been noticed, except by Mr. Halliwell, in his *Round-
about Notes* (1863). He thinks, however, that stone avenues
existed; but this seems doubtful. There are, indeed, one or
two irregularities in the exterior of the circle, which may have
been caused by later kists added on the outside. He is, however, not far from right in thinking it to be *"perhaps the most
curious sepulchral monument in Great Britain."*

From the regularity with which the graves have been arranged
in pairs, and the complete similarity of the kists themselves, ·
they appear to have been the work of the same hands, and of
the same time. Other graves are said to exist on the mountain,
but not arranged as these are. It is, however, certain that
no careful examination has yet been made of the ground, an
omission which it is to be hoped will soon be rectified. Immediate steps should at any rate be taken to surround this group
with a wall to prevent its destruction, for although the kists
are individually of no great importance, yet their being thus
grouped together gives them a value, which it is to be hoped
will be appreciated by the proprietors of the land.

The other stone remains visited during the meeting of the
Cambrian Association are of the later kind, and must be referred to Scandinavian occupiers of the island.

In a field near the Tynwald Mount were three kistvaens, one
of which was laid bare by a cutting through the road, and examined during one of the excursions of the week. This had
evidently been buried within the ground, to some depth, as will
be seen from the accompanying illustration. At the time of its
discovery nothing was found within it, so that it may have been
rifled on a former occasion. Near it were the two other similar
graves, close to one another,—one of which contained a battle-

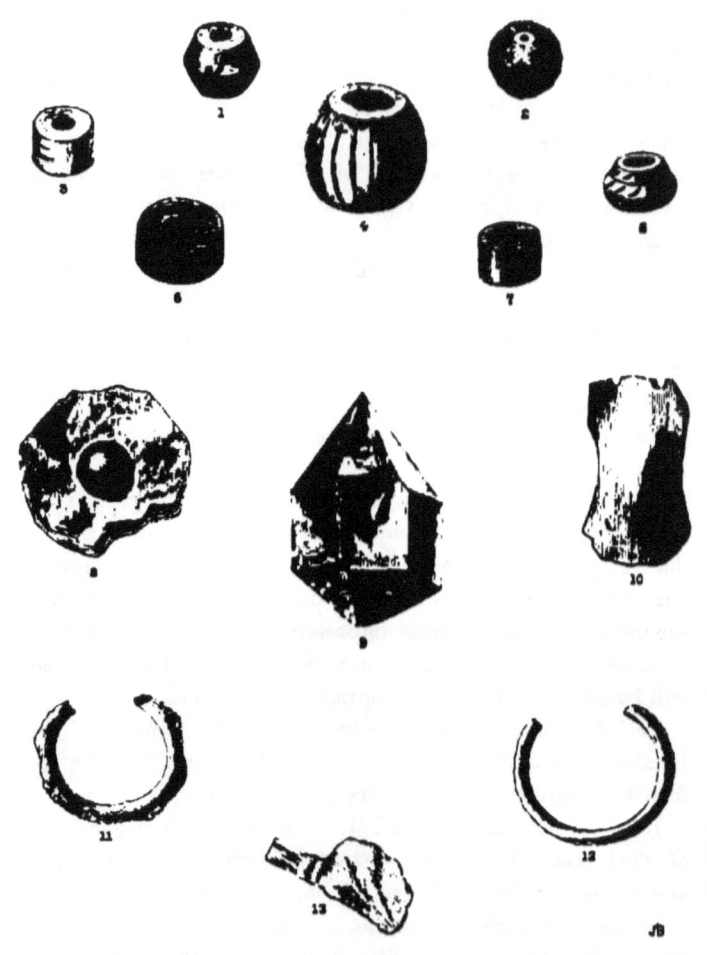

BEADS, ROCK CRYSTAL, AND ORNAMENTS, FOUND IN A KISTVAEN NEAR
ST. JOHN'S TYNWALD MOUNT, ISLE OF MAN.

axe and spur, the other a collection of beads and other ornaments and an urn. What has become of the former is not
ascertained ; the others are in the Museum of Practical Geo-
logy in Jermyn Street. That the three kists are of the same
character and age there can be little doubt ; and that they were
Scandinavian is shown by the relics of two of them. A correct
account of these important discoveries is given in a letter from
Mr. F. Matthews to Dr. Oliver, which will be found in the
Notes to the *Vestigia*. As it was in this and the adjoining
fields that a battle took place between Olave and his brother
Reginald, and in which the latter was slain, that there was some
connexion between the battle and these graves is very probable. The relics are those of a person of importance ; but
not of Reginald himself, since his body was taken by the monks
of Rushen Abbey and buried in the Abbey of Furness.

The objects in Jermyn Street, since examined and drawn by
Mr. Blight, are represented in the engraving by that gentleman.

No. 1. Yellow glass bead with red markings.

No. 2. Glass bead with facets dark blue.

No. 3. Opaque white glass bead.

No. 4. Turquoise coloured blue bead, larger than the others.

No. 5. Yellow glass bead with dark blue markings.

No. 6. Bead similar in form to No. 3, resembling Samian
ware.

No. 7. Blue glass bead similar in form to No. 3.

No. 8. Dark blue glass set in copper nearly converted into
metal carbonate.

No. 9. Rock crystal.

No. 10. A portion of an ornament of silver, much oxydised.

No. 11. Portion of a copper ring.

No. 12. Portion of a silver ring nearly converted into chlo-
ride or horn silver.

No. 13. Fragment probably of an ornament, and which seems
to be metal.

The group in Kirklonan parish, on the Minorca road, between Ramsey and Douglas, is popularly known as King
Orry's grave. The name is associated with other places in
the island, as at Bishop's Court, where the mediæval tower is
called Orry's tower. Orrisdale is in the same locality. King
Orry's son and successor died in 954. There appears, however,
to have been more than one grave, as the existing remains
show. The group was opened some thirty years ago, when it
was found to contain a dome vaulted chamber, which itself
contained a kistvaen, as if especial honour had been intended by
this peculiar arrangement. A mere covering of earth or stones
would have been sufficient for the purpose, as was the usual
practice. In this case, a vaulted chamber had been added.
Professor Simpson has remarked a somewhat similar instance
of this double enclosure. In the cromlech on the mountain near
Harlech, associated with the name of Arthur, he noticed that a
kistvaen had been placed within the cromlech itself. But such
instances are very rare. When Orry's grave was opened, it
contained a few human bones, the skeleton of a horse, an iron
horse-shoe (now in the possession of Mr. Paul Bridson), and
an iron sword,—objects which indubitably point to a Scandinavian interment. How the chamber was vaulted is omitted in
the account. If the vaulting, so-called, was not effected by
stones overlapping one another, but in the usual manner of
ordinary vaulting, the monument cannot be of very ancient
character.*

The Cloven Stones of Laxey, nearer Douglas, are the remains of another grave with its surrounding pillar-stones. In
Wood's *Isle of Man* (1811) the author states he saw twelve
stones placed in an oval form on the mount. If this account
be correct, the position of the stones on the mount, as in the
Arragon circle, would indicate the structure to be Scandina-

* Mr. David Forbes states that the late Mr. Frank Matthews forwarded
to his late brother, Professor Forbes, the sword found in Orry's grave; but
of its subsequent fate he is ignorant.

vian. Local tradition terms it the burial-place of a Welsh prince who reigned on the island between the seventh and eighth centuries. It is more probably the resting-place of a Norseman.

Another work is associated with Orry's name, called Castle Chorry, lying still nearer Ramsay. This was not visited; but from the representation of it given in Mr. Cumming's larger work, it appears to be a simple sepulchral circle, retaining in the interior some of the stones which once composed the interior cave or chamber.

The large and small kists in the grounds of Orrisdale, have been removed for the sake of security to their present position. Nothing was found in the larger one but a confused entangled mass of vegetable matter containing small white particles, which appear to have come from burnt bone. The smaller kist is square, and of such small dimensions that it could only have held ashes, or the doubled-up body of a small child. Numerous similar kists are said to exist on the hill from which these were brought.

Cronk ny Keeillane is on a hill cut through by the high road, near Peel, and has been well described in the appendix to Oswald's *Vestigia*. The mound was raised originally upon the summit of a rising ground, and has been the nucleus of an important cemetery, as graves have been frequently disturbed by the plough. The kistvaens, that have been opened, are built of thin slabs of slaty rag stones, and are of an humble and meagre character. The bodies appear to have been placed in one uniform position, nearly east and west. The skull, which had been cut through by some trenchant implement, and which was exhibited in the Museum, was taken from one of the kists. An old Treen church stood on the plateau above the graves that were opened, but all traces of its site are gone. Whether the original church preceded or was subsequent to the interments, is an interesting point; for if subsequent, it would shew that this spot had been chosen as a cemetery from very

early times, although the character of the present graves is
somewhat dubious. But whether Christian or not, they may
have succeeded still earlier ones; so that, as in the case of
Ballamona cemetery, we may have an instance of a cemetery
dating from the earliest period to a comparatively recent one.
Connected with the Treen chapel was a Runic cross, never described, which, during a murrain among the cattle of the district,
acquired a bad character amongst the natives as being connected with the disease. It was accordingly buried in the
ground, and no persuasion to disclose the spot has yet been
effective. The man, who did the act, still lives, but keeps the
secret,—all the less likely to be known at the time, when the
rinderpest existed on the opposite shore. If that plague should
ever find its way into the island, perhaps other Runic monuments may disappear.

The other stone remains which exist throughout the island
will be probably found to be similar to one or other of the
classes here briefly touched upon. St. Patrick's chair, at
Magher-y-Chiarn, in Marown Parish, of a somewhat different
character, may, perhaps, have been the modern fabrication of
a neighbouring farmer, who may have found (if he did not
manufacture them) these stones in different spots, and grouped
them thus together, either from some whim, or to prevent
their interference with his plough. They were not, however,
seen by the members of the Association during their visit to
the island; so their real history must be left for Manx
archæologists.

PATEN, KIRK MALEW, ISLE OF MAN.

VIII.

CHURCH FURNITURE IN MALEW CHURCH, ISLE OF MAN.

BY THE REV. F. L. BARNWELL.

During the visit of the Association to the Isle of Man, in 1865, a visit was made to Malew Church, which the Rev. J. G. Cumming considers a good specimen of the older Manx churches. There is nothing very remarkable about the building, except a roof of the thirteenth century, and a small rude granite font of uncertain date. The church, however, possesses certain articles of church furniture of unusual interest, namely, a silver paten, a bronze crucifix, a portion of a staff covered with brass, and a curious bronze article, described in some of the guide-books as an extinguisher.

The paten is represented in the cut, from a careful drawing and a rubbing; for the latter of which the Association is indebted to Mr. Adcock of Birmingham. The face has a somewhat rude, archaic appearance, probably arising from a deficiency of artistic skill; but the other details clearly point to the early part of the fifteenth century. The legend is, SANCTE LUPE ORA PRO NODIS; thus confirming, according to Mr. Cumming, the derivation of the name of the church (Malew) from "Ma", saint, and "Lupus"; as Marown, a neighbouring parish, is so called from "Ma-Rooney". St. Lupus was bishop of Troyes.

The second object is a bronze crucifix. On reference to the adjoining cut it will be seen that the lower part of the body is enveloped in a folded garment, secured at the hip by a ring or button.   This garment has not the appearance of ordinary drapery.   The upper portion of the body is covered with a vest with sleeves concealing the arms, perhaps no farther than the

Crucifix. Kirk Malew, Isle of Man.

fracture, a little below the elbow; for, unfortunately, the figure has lost the extremities of the arms and legs.   The vest is so short that the middle of the body lies exposed between

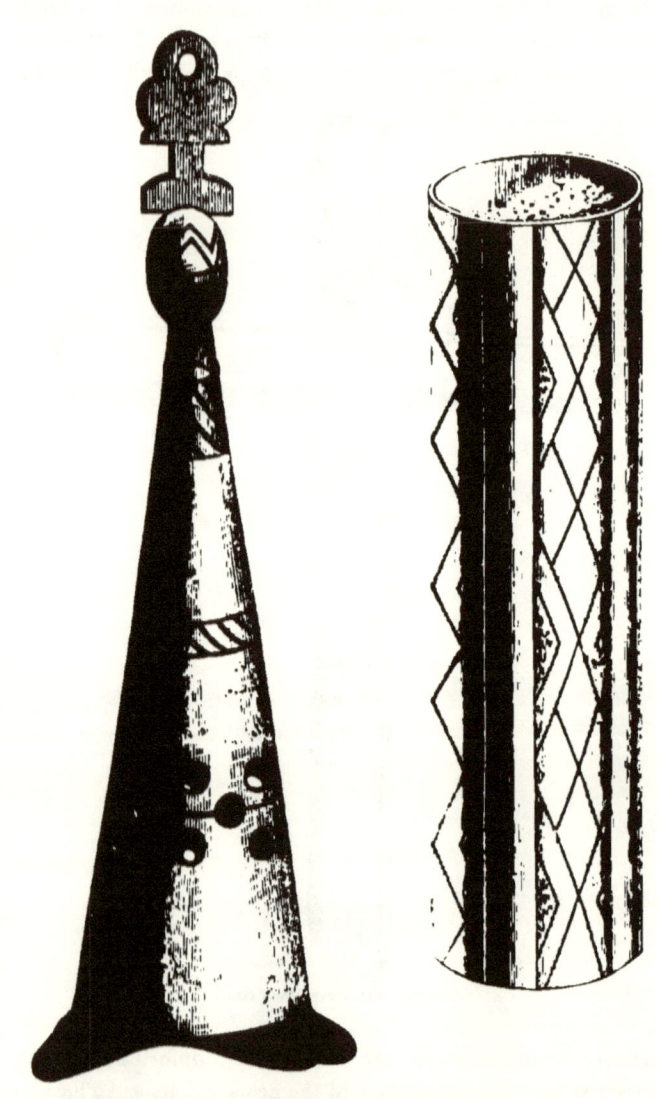

KIRK MALEW, ISLE OF MAN.

the two vestments, an unusual arrangement. It is stated that, anterior to the eleventh century, the body of Christ was covered with a sleeved mantle; while during that and the following century, the lower part only of the body was concealed by a short jupon. The present example appears to have been a kind of combination of the two practices. The elongated head, of Byzantine character, the crown of twisted rope, and the position of the legs, which were not generally crossed until the thirteenth century, are all indications of the age of the crucifix, namely, the twelfth century. The peculiar, triangular form of the cross, ornamented with a kind of bead, and the four streams of blood descending down the forehead, should be noticed.

The portion of a staff covered with brass is called in some of the guide-books a candlestick, to which, however, it bears no resemblance. It may be the remains of the shaft of a processional cross; or, what is not unlikely, it may be connected with the very singular article (see cut) which has hitherto been called an extinguisher, although the small apertures clearly shew it was nothing of the kind, in spite of its tapering form. Some present during the visit conjectured it to have been the cover of a thurible of very unusual type; but the phlanges at the lower part shew that it had been permanently fastened. The conjecture of the Right Rev. Dr. Goss, however, no doubt solves the question satisfactorily, who thinks it must have been the top of a lantern suspended from a pole, and borne before the priests while conveying the host to sick parishioners. The shape, the holes, the phlanges, all combine to render this supposition very probable; and it is not impossible that the fragment of the staff just mentioned, may have been a portion of the pole to which the lantern was suspended. There is a certain similarity in the ornamentation of both articles, shewing that they are nearly of the same date, which may be as early as that of the fourteenth century; but the pattern is of that simple character which is not easily assignable to any particular period.

Mr. Cumming, in his excellent *Guide*, mentions an ancient chalice; which was not, however, exhibited at the time. It is described as being very small, little larger than what is used at present for private Communion. A legend, however, is connected with it, according to the marvel-loving Waldron, who tells us that the fairies once gave to a benighted traveller *on barule*, a cup, which the then parson of Malew persuaded the lucky traveller to hand over to his church; and which, according to Waldron, was used as the chalice in his time. But however this may be, the island is fortunate in possessing a very fine chalice, probably of the fourteenth century, which is here given. It belongs to Jurby Church, and is copied from a drawing kindly lent with the other drawings by the Rev. J. Simpson of Douglas. (See plate.)

It is very satisfactory to know that these various relics are properly valued, and carefully guarded, by the clergymen of the two parishes. Those of Malew Church were until lately kept in a box under the pulpit; but have since been properly removed to the house of the present incumbent, whose refusal to the members of the Association, on that occasion, to let them be removed for a night, for the purpose of being drawn, was as determined as commendable. However, the difficulty was met by the kindness of Mr. Simpson in lending the Association his own drawings, the accuracy of which will be at once recognised by those who examined the objects themselves on the occasion of the Meeting.

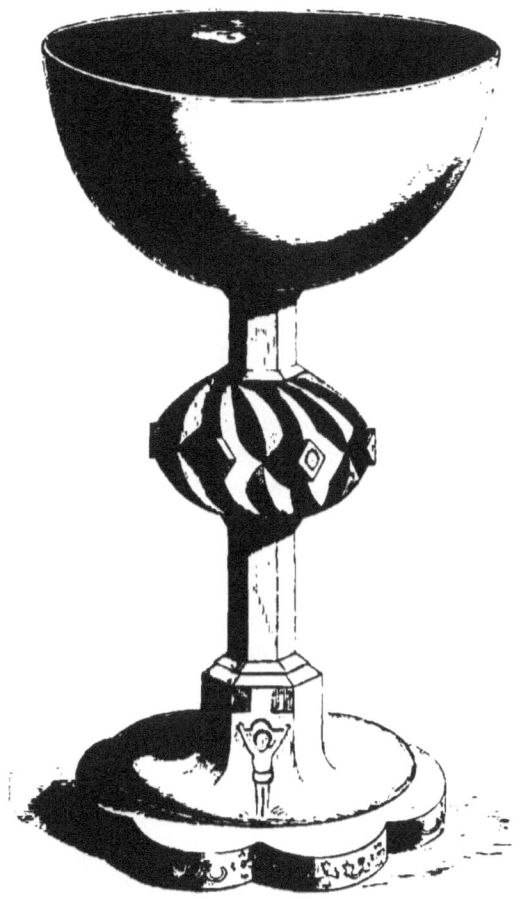

CHALICE FROM THE PARISH CHURCH OF JURBY, ISLE OF MAN.

IX.

UNCERTAIN BRONZE IMPLEMENTS, ISLE OF MAN.

BY THE REV. E. L. BARNWELL.

IN the Temporary Museum at Douglas, during the Meeting of the Association in the Isle of Man last year, there was exhibited a stone mould, of which an accurate representation is here given from the pencil of Mr. Blight. The stone is at King William's College. In the catalogue of the Museum it was said to be a mould for casting combs; but it is doubtful if combs of such a form have ever been discovered,—at any rate such a three-pronged article seems ill adapted for such a purpose. The earliest combs in wood or bone are of very different form : in fact, they are almost the same as those in use at the present day. Men sufficiently advanced so as to practise the art of casting metal would hardly have adopted such a form if they wanted a comb. It may, therefore, be safely assumed that the article in question is nothing of the kind. It is, however, not so easy to say what it is, and what its use. It bears, indeed, a faint resemblance to the bronze implement lately found in Anglesey, and described in a late number of the *Archæologia Cambrensis* by Mr. Albert Way. That implement, which is very similar to one found in Edinburgh, and noticed in the *Proceedings* of the Scottish Antiquaries, is supposed to have been a kind of razor. Similar articles have also been found in Ireland ; but none of these is of the same form as the one under consideration, which could not, from the narrow space between the prongs, admit of the finger and thumb, by which the razors were thought to have been held.

The circular mould also presents another difficulty; for it is not easy to guess at its intended use, and whether the disc of cast metal was in any way connected with the three-pronged instrument. The presence, however, of the two moulds on one block seems to shew that these may have had some connexion.

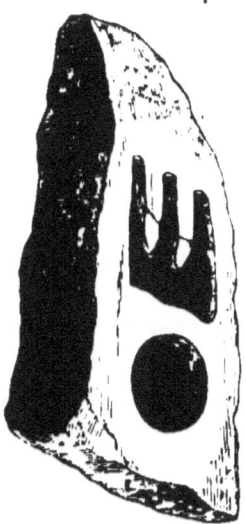 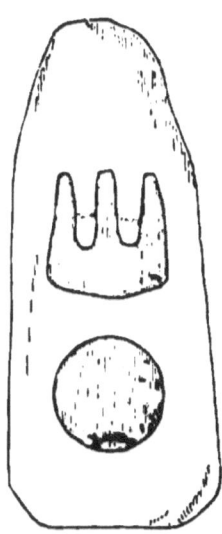

The larger of the two implements may, however, have served as a veritable fork, which may have been fitted with a double handle; but in this case one would have expected that it would have been provided with a tang or shaft of some kind; or it may have been a kind of scraper, although this suggestion is worth little. It is possible that similar articles may exist in some collection, by a comparison of which some light may be thrown on what at present seems to be a puzzle.

X.

CIRCLE ON "THE MULL," ISLE OF MAN.

BY J. M. JEFFCOTT, ESQ., H.K.

ONE of the most remarkable monuments of antiquity on the
island is a circle on the mountain called "The Mule," or "The
Mull," in the parish of Rushen. It is situated on a rocky emi-
nence about midway between Port Erin and the hamlet of
Cregneese.* The spot is wild and desolate, and has probably
undergone little change since the circle was first formed. In
the immediate vicinity of the structure is a valley which abounds
with crags and slaty stones. From this valley is derived its
local name, "Rhullick y lagg shliggagh;" i.e., "the graveyard
of the valley of broken slates." I had much difficulty in ascertaining its name, for which I am indebted to two aged natives
who live at Cregneese: indeed, had it not been for the information afforded by these venerable islesmen, the name would in
all probability have been lost. The noun *shlig* means shell,
shred, or fragment; and my informants explain the adjective
shliggagh as having reference to the pieces of stone or slate
usually found about a quarry.

An engraving from a drawing which I had made of this
circle accompanied the Rev. E. L. Barnwell's "Notes on the
Stone Monuments of the Isle of Man," in the number of the

---

* This is, perhaps, the oldest and most primitive of the existing hamlets
of the island, and is formed chiefly of thatched cottages. *Creg*, in the Manx
dialect, signifies "rock"; and *neese*, in the same dialect, means "below."
Hence the name of the village denotes its position, "below the rock."

Archæologia Cambrensis for January 1866, and is given on page 101 *supra*. The circle is formed of kistvaens arranged singly : throughout the whole ring two cannot be found placed side by side. Some of them are nearly entire ; and of these, the imposts only are wanting. The grey, flat stones of which they are composed were, doubtless, originally obtained close to the place where they now stand. Several of the stones are

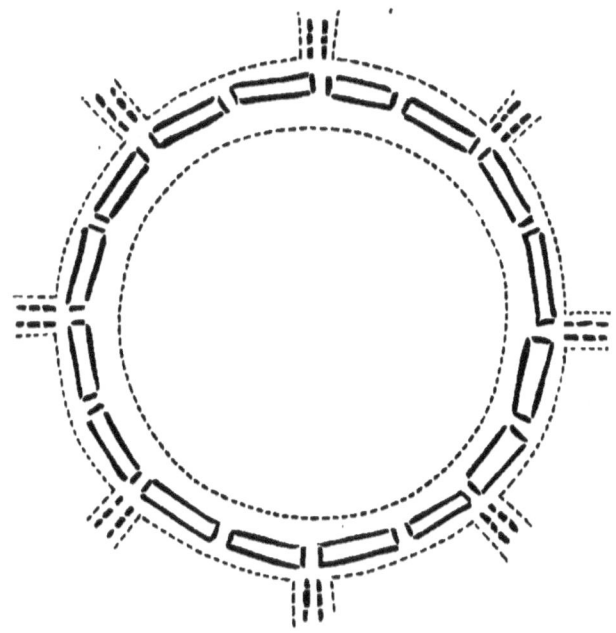

Plan of Circle on the Mull, Isle of Man.

seven feet long, and some are upwards of three feet high. They vary in thickness from six to sixteen inches, and are of a very rude character. The width of the spaces which they enclose varies from thirty-four inches to three feet seven inches.

This monument has one novel feature deserving of special

notice.   At different points two rows of stones are placed parallel to each other, outside of, and diverging from, the circle.   These, at first sight, might appear to indicate passages into the interior; but after several careful examinations of the remains, I have no hesitation in saying that the spaces which they inclose were not openings into the structure, nor were they kists.   The stones are unquestionably in their original position.   The spaces enclosed by the several rows are nowhere more than two feet wide; and, though opposite the vacancies between the ends of the kistvaens, such vacancies seem to have been, at least in two instances, not more than fourteen or sixteen inches wide, and therefore too narrow to have been used as entrances.   The kistvaens were originally covered with turf and soil, combined, probably, with fragments of stone; and, with their covering, formed, I believe, a circular bank or an elevated ring.   The present appearance of the structure indicates clearly the former existence of an annular embankment; and when this was entire, the narrow openings between the ends of the kistvaens must have been closed. Moreover, if the spaces, which I have described, were entrances or avenues, why do they project five or six feet from the circle?   The manner in which the stones are placed does not warrant us in assuming that they formed kistvaens.   Their character is distinct from that of the stones of which the kistvaens in the circle are composed.

The double rows of stones were eight in number: four of these rows faced very nearly the four points of the compass, and the others divided equally the intervening portions of the circle, in the manner represented in the accompanying plan.

Four are still distinctly visible : one opposite the west, and another the north-west : one opposite the north-east, and another the south.   These diverging rows of stones must, I think, have been originally built upon, and have given to the circle, when entire, an asteriated appearance.   The structure may, perhaps, have been intended to represent a star or the sun.

Is it not possible that the sun and stars were objects of worship among the primeval occupants of the island?

Sepulchral mounds and circles are of very frequent occurrence in Man, and might seem to point to the existence, at a very remote period, of a dense population. There is, however, no reason for the belief that the early inhabitants were numerous. The monuments themselves are generally of very limited size. The circle which I have described could not, I think, have contained more than eighteen kists; and, indeed, the actual number may not have exceeded sixteen. It was, perhaps, used by only one family; or it may have been the joint property of a few families dwelling in close proximity to each other. At a comparatively recent date, soon after the introduction of Christianity into the island, and anterior to its division into parishes, numerous families had, it seems, their respective cemeteries, on which they erected, of sods and stones, rude and diminutive chapels. (See Dr. Oliver's paper, *supra*.)

I have been informed that fragments of human bones have been taken from the kistvaens on the Mull. Most probably these bones had been partially burned, but unless others be discovered the fact cannot now be ascertained. Any cinerary urns, which may have been deposited in the kists, must long since have been destroyed. It might be interesting to excavate within the circle, but it is hardly likely that any valuable discovery could by excavation be made. Its whole area is covered only by a small quantity of soil; the kistvaens stand upon rock.

The early sepulchral monuments of the island seem to have belonged to different periods, for they are not all of the same class. There is one class which differs very materially from that to which the circle already described belongs. I refer to that composed of tumuli capped with great masses of quartz. A tumulus of this sort occurs in the neighbourhood of Orry's Dale, in the parish of Michael. On the summit of the mound, which is partially a natural one, huge stones, each weighing

upwards of a ton, are arranged in the form of a circle. These
ponderous stones are supposed to have been brought from the
bed of Sulby River, a distance of five or six miles; for no such
stones, it is thought, ever existed in the neighbourhood of the
tumulus. I have no doubt that they were, in their present
position, once covered with turf and soil; and there is still on
one of the stones a heap of earth. Cinerary urns have been
found in this tumulus. The differences in the form and character of the Manx tumuli lead to the conclusion that they were
not the works of one tribe. Small Allophylian colonies were
doubtless occasionally formed in the island, and they introduced
among the primordial inhabitants foreign customs and a foreign
idolatry. The frequent occurrence of ancient tumuli and circles
within a short distance from the sea renders it probable that
the aboriginal possessors of the land usually dwelt in creeks
and bays, where they were more likely to obtain subsistence
than in the interior of the country.

It would be interesting to know for a certainty to what use
the spaces within the circles, whether formed of kistvaens, or
solid masses of stone, were applied. It is exceedingly probable
that within such enclosed spaces the bodies of the dead were
subjected to the process of cremation. It can hardly be supposed that there were not certain places where the practice
was invariably carried out. We know that in the later times
of the republic, when the custom obtained among the Romans,
they had their *ustrinæ*, where cremation was performed.

In further illustration of the subject of the foregoing paper,
it may be stated that the arranging of kistvaens (*cistveini*) in
circles is, though rare, not without parallel in Wales. Not far
from Newport, in Pembrokeshire, there is a collection of five
kistvaens, or small cromlechs, arranged in a circle; not, indeed, on the circumference, but radiating from the centre :
that is to say, there is an evident approximation to this form.

One idea, however, started by Mr. Jeffcott is novel, and yet well worthy of careful remark; viz., that the kistvaens along the circumference were once all covered by a continuous ridge of earth, forming a kind of embankment. Now we find in Wales, and, I believe in Britanny, numerous examples of circles composed of a continuous embankment; but hitherto, I believe, no kistvaens have been found within these embankments. It would, therefore, be worth while to probe, *not to destroy*, some embankments of this nature, in order to see whether they covered any places of sepulture.

With regard to the kistvaens themselves, they seem to resemble what we find commonly both above and below ground in Wales; but the rows of stones radiating from the outside of the circumference would seem to be altogether peculiar. The nature of the soil beneath these stones, being rocky, certainly damps the expectation of finding sepulchral remains connected with such a circle as that on the Mull; still search should be made, and conducted with all precautions calculated to ensure the preservation of this interesting monument of early Manx-men.

It is curious that no Roman remains should yet have been pointed out on the island; for it is hardly possible that the conquerors of Britain should not have known, and even established their supremacy over it. Possibly future discoveries may solve this part of the problem of Manx history.

H. L. J.

XI.

MANANAN MAC LIR: HIS MYTHIC CONNEXION WITH THE ISLE OF MAN.

BY RICHARD R. BRASH, M.R.I.A.

THE original discovery and peopling of our European islands are enveloped in the mists of fable and tradition. Saturn, Jupiter, and Minos are said to have been early kings of Crete; Phorcus, a descendant of Noah, to have peopled Sardinia. Sicilian chronologists deduce the pedigrees of the Sicilians from Gomer, the son of Japhet, whom they assert to have peopled that island a short time after the flood. Brutus and his Trojans are fabled to have found their way to these islands, and to have given a name to Britain. The Irish Seanachuidhe attributes the colonisation of Ireland to Partho-lanus, a descendant of Magog, the son of Japhet, three hundred years after the flood; while Man, not to be outdone by these greater rivals, claims for itself a truly ancient and fabulous colonisation.

The subject I have taken up in connection with the Isle of Man is an exclusively mythic one. Mananan Mac Lir cannot claim an historical existence; nevertheless his name and attributes are so mixed up with the written romance, and traditionary lore of Ireland, that the possible existence of some personage who formed the foundation of these ancient tales, is more than probable.

The origin of the geographical name, Man, has been a puzzle to the historian and antiquary. The learned Camden gives

the names by which it was known to ancient authors. He
writes,—" Ptolemy calls it ' Monoeda quasi *Moneitha*' ; *i.e.*, if
I may be allowed a conjecture, *Further Mona*, to distinguish it
from the other Mona ; Pliny, Monabia ; Orosius, Mevania ;
and Bede, Menavia Secunda, where he calls Mona (or Anglesey)
Menavia Prima, and both British islands." In the Irish version of Nennius it is called Eubonia and Manau. In an ancient MS. in the Harleian Collections, quoted in the *Cam.
Quart. May.*, iv, p. 23, Man is styled Manan Guodotin.

From the foregoing it is evident that the names Manan,
Man, are the foundation of all the above appellations ; but
whence this root, and by whom originally applied ? Here
Irish traditionary lore steps in, and supplies the clue when it
states that this island derives its name from Mananan Mac Lir,
or " Mananan the son of the sea," a celebrated navigator and
merchant who made Man the chief depôt of his trade. Gough,
in his additions to *Camden*, notices this tradition when he
states, it makes " the first owner of this island to have been
Mananan Mac Leir, a magician, who kept it enveloped in perpetual mist till St. Patrick broke the charm." *Ler* or *leur* (the
sea), genitive *lir*, is an Irish word still in general use. In
Bullock's history of the Isle of Man, the above tradition is thus
introduced from the Manx Statute Book: "Mananan Mac Leir
(the first man who held Man), was ruler thereof, and after
whom the land was named, reigned many years, and was a
paynim. He kept the land under mists by his necromancy.
If he dreaded an enemy, he would of one man cause to seem
an hundred, and that by art magic." Sacheverel, in his account of Man, notices the same myth.

Before entering on the Irish traditions of this personage, it
would be well to notice the close connection existing between
Ireland and Man from the remotest ages. Æthicus, the cos-
mographer, asserts that the Isle of Man as well as Ireland was
peopled by the Scoti, " Menavia insula æque ac Hibernia a
Scotorum gentibus habitatur." Orosius makes a similar state-

ment,—" Britanniæ spatio terrarum augustior sed cœli colitur. Hinc etiam Mevania insula proxima est et ipsa spatio non parva solo commoda æque a Scotorum gentibus habitatur." (*Cambrensis Eversus*, vol. i, p. 159.) According to the Irish annalist, Tighernac, Cormac, the son of Con Cead-Catha (of the hundred battles), in A.D. 254 expatriated a number of his rebellious subjects, Ultonians, and compelled them to emigrate into Man. From thence he was called Cormac Ulfada. The learned editor of the Irish version of Nennius adopts the opinion that the expelled Ultonians were Irish Picts or Crutheni. We have, however, traces of an earlier occupation of Man, as is stated in the work above cited,—" But the Firbolgi seized upon Man and certain islands in like manner, Ara, Ili, and Rachra.* (Irish Arch. Soc. Pub., Dublin, 1848, p. 49.) The Firbolgs were the colonists who preceded the Tuaths de Danans and Milesians in the occupation of Ireland.

Camden, Usher, Lhuyd, and Pinkerton, all acknowledge the Manx to be descended from the Hibernian Scoti. The languages are admitted by philologists to be identical, with the exception of such variations as local causes, and a strong Scandinavian element would produce.

The topographical nomenclature of Man is intensely Irish [? *Celtic.* Ed.] The Rev. Isaac Taylor, in his admirable work, *Words and Places,* upon this subject has the following passage: "The ethnology of the Isle of Man may be very completely illustrated by means of local names. The map of the island contains about four hundred names, of which about twenty per cent. are English, twenty-one per cent. are Norwegian, and *fifty-nine per cent. are Celtic.* These Celtic names are all of the most characteristic Erse type. It would appear that not a single colonist from Wales ever reached the island,† which from the mountains

* Arran, Islay, and Rathlin.

† The Isle of Man was governed by princes from North Wales for the space of four centuries. The first was Maelgwyn, who conquered the island A.D. 525, and the last, Anarawd ap Roderic, who died A.D. 913. (J. R. O.)

of Caernarvon is seen like a faint cloud upon the blue waters."
There are ninety-six names beginning with Balla ; and the
names of more than a dozen of the highest mountains have the
prefix Sliew, answering to the Irish Slievh or Sliabh. The
Isle of Man has the Curraghs, the Loughs, and the Allens of
Ireland faithfully reproduced. It is curious that the names
which denote places of Christian worship are all Norwegian.
They are an indication of the late date at which heathenism
must have prevailed."

It is a curious and suggestive fact that the fossil deer of
Ireland is found nowhere out of that island except in Man.* On
the 3rd of September, 1856, a communication was read before
the Kilkenny Archæological Society by Mr. Edward Benn of
Liverpool, advocating the theory of the contemporary existence
of man and the *Megaceros Hibernicus*, or gigantic fossil deer of
Ireland. He writes,—" I have also stated that they are known
to Ireland only ; but to this there is a very remarkable exception, as they have been discovered in the Isle of Man, at a
place called Ballaugh. The circumstances attending their discovery there are quite similar to those in Lecale in Down,
except that the number of skeletons, compared with heads, is
relatively greater in the former than in the Irish locality. The
place where they are found in Man, which is in the north-west
part of the island, just opposite Lecale, had formerly been a
lake ; and in maps of even two hundred and fifty years ago,
large lakes are marked as being at this place where none now
exist. . . . . . Another curious question is, How did so large an
animal come to inhabit so small a place as the Isle of Man ?
Was it a separate creation ? This is out of the question. Was
it brought there by human intervention ? This is nearly as
improbable. Did it swim or travel on ice ? This also seems

* This statement requires correction. Many examples have been found
in England: in caves, as in Kent's Hole; in peat bogs, in Lancashire; at
Hilgay, Norfolk; at Walton in Essex; and in an oyster-bed at Happisburgh.
See Owen's *History of British Fossil Mammals and Birds.* The first perfect
specimen was found near Ballaugh, Isle of Man. (Editor, J. G. C.)

an improbable conjecture. I think tho circumstance is one of the proofs that this island was once united to Ireland, and not to England or Scotland.* Besides the existence of the remains of tho Irish elk, many other things unite to confirm this conjecture. The inhabitants bear strong points of resemblance to tho Irish; the zoology is identical; the absence of moles, toads, and all the serpent tribe, point it out as almost a part of Ireland; and the circumstance of the Irish hare being found in it, tends to make the resemblance still closer."

The epoch of the actual separation is, perhaps, not so very far distant as we might imagine. There is a current tradition both in Ireland and the Isle of Man, that in "the wars of the giants one took up a handful of earth which he threw at another, but missed his aim. The place from which the handful of earth was lifted became Lough Neagh, and that at which it fell the Isle of Man."

In tho topographical poem of O'Heerin reference is made to Man by way of comparison,—

"Is the plain of Manainn fairer?"

In a poem contained in the book of Leacan it is stated of Baedan McCairill, King of Ulster,—"It was by him that . Manainn was cleared of the Galls (foreigners), so that its sovereignty belonged to the Ultonians from thence forward." Baedan died A.D. 580. (*Cambrensis Eversus,* Irish Celtic Soc., Dublin, 1848, vol. i, p. 165.) In the chapter of wonders contained in the Irish version of Nennius we have,—"The wonders of Manann down here. The first wonder is a strand without a sea; the second is a ford which is far from the sea, and which fills when the tide flows, and decreases when the tide ebbs; the third is a stone which moves at night in Glenn Cindenn; and though it should be cast into the sea, or into a cataract, it would be found on the margin of the same valley."

In the enumeration of the various tributes payable by the

* There is just as distinct proof that it was united to England and Scotland. See Memoir by the Rev. J. G. Cumming, "On tho Area of the Irish Sea", Vol. i, *Edinbro' New Philosophical Journal.* (Editor.)

inferior kings and chieftains to the King of Tara, as set forth
in the *Book of Rights*, we have included "the fruits of Manann,
a fine present." (*Book of Rights*, Celtic Soc., Dub., 1847, p. 9.)

Mananan Mac Lir, the supposed coloniser and first ruler of
Man, or Manan, and from which he derives his name, was
identical with the merchant or navigator Orbsen, so celebrated
in Irish bardic history, and from whom Lough Orbsen (now
Corrib in Galway), was named. He is thus introduced to our
notice by the learned author of the *Ogygia*,—" The merchant
Orbsen was remarkable for carrying on a commercial intercourse between Ireland and Britain. He was commonly called
Mananan Mac Lir,—that is, Mananan on account of his intercourse with the Isle of Man ; and Mac Lir ; *i.e., sprung from
the sea*, because he was an export diver; besides, he understood the dangerous parts of harbours; and, from his pre-
science of the change of weather, always avoided tempests."
(*Ogygia*, Dublin edit., 1793, p. 26.) The genealogy of Mananan is given in Keating. "Mananan, the son of Alladh, the
son of Elathan, son of Dalboeth, son of Neidh, an immediate
descendent of Nemedius, the progenitor of the Tuatha de
Danans in Ireland ; that weird and mystic colony who never,
through the lapse of ages, have relinquished their dominion
over the superstitions of the peasantry of Ireland ; but who
are still believed to rule the spirit or fairy land of Erin ; to
reign paramount in the lis, the cave, the mine; to occupy
genii palaces in the deepest recesses of mountains, and under
the deep waters of our lakes." Keating further states, the
proper name of Orbsen was Mananan ; that from him the lake
was called, because when his grave was digging the lake
broke forth. This myth respecting the breaking forth of lakes
is quite common in Ireland. There is scarcely a sheet of water
in the country that has not a tale relating the cause, or incident
connected with its breaking forth. The formation of almost
all the larger lakes is mentioned in the *Annals*.

In the time of O'Flaherty, the learned author of the *Ogygia*,

Lough Corrib was then called Lough Orbsen. This was in the middle of the seventeenth century. In his work on West Connaught he thus refers to it, as well as to the field of Magh Ullin (now Moycullin), where Mananan, or Orbsen, was slain. "Gnobeg contains the parishes of Moycullin and Rahun. The three first parishes lie in length from Lough Orbsen to the Bay of Galway, and Rahun from the River of Galway to the same bay. The castle and manor of Moycullin, whence the barony and parish are named, hath Lough Lonon on the west; Tolokian, two castles next adjacent, on the north; and Lough Orbsen on the east. . . . Here Uillinn, grandchild of Nuadh (silver-hand), King of Ireland twelve hundred years before Christ's birth, overthrew in battle, and had the killing of, Orbsen Mac Alloid, commonly called Mananan (the Mankish man), Mac Lir (son of the sea), for his skill in seafaring. From Uillinn, Moycullin is named,—to wit, Magh-Ullin, the field of Ullin; and from Orbsen, Lough Orbsen, or the lake of Orbsen. Six miles from a great stone in that field (erected, perhaps, in memory of the same battle) is the town of Galway." (*West Connaught*, by the *Irish Arch. Soc., Dublin*, 1846, p. 54.) The corruption of the name Orbsen to Corrib is easy and evident,—Orbsen, Oreb, Orib, Corrib. Cormac MacCullennain, king and bishop of Cashel A.D. 901, in his *Glossary*, thus notices this personage: "Manannan Mac Lir, a famous merchant who dwelt in the Isle of Man. He was the greatest navigator of this western part of the world, and used to presage good or bad weather from his observations of the heavens, and from the changes of the moon; wherefore the Scots, *i.e.*, the Irish and Britons, gave him the title of ' god of the sea'. They also called him Mac Lir, that is, *the son of the sea*, and from him the Isle of Man had its name." (Ibid., p. 21.)

The name of this personage is seldom mentioned in the traditionary tales and folk-lore of Ireland without Druidic and fairy associations. He is generally esteemed a good genius, powerful in magic spells and enchantments, usually exercised

for benevolent purposes. He is sometimes represented as
coming from Armenia, and as having returned thither after the
introduction of Christianity. In some instances he is described
as a Canaanite. Irish myths invariably point to the east, and
more particularly single out those parts which were originally
the seat of primæval man. The countries bordering on the
Caspian, Iran, Turan, Armenia, are localities from whence
Irish romantic tradition brings her heroes and hero-gods, and
to which she often sends them in search of adventures. Each
division of Ireland had its fairy king. Mananan is stated to
have ruled over the Ulster genii, Crop over those of Connaught,
Don Firrinn over those of Munster. The palace of Mananan
was fabled to have been on the brink of a lake near Enniskeen,
county of Monaghan.

In a curious historical tract entitled *The Fate of the Sons of
Tuirinn*, which describes the slavery imposed upon Nuadh of
the Silver Hand and the Tuath de Danans by the Fomorians,
or African pirates, as they are designated in Irish mythic
history, and supposed by many learned antiquaries to indicate
a colony of Carthaginian traders or adventurers who, at some
period unascertained, frequented the coasts of Ireland for
trade, and to whom are attributed the introduction of those
curious leaf-shaped bronze swords so frequently found in Ireland as well as in the sister country, and which have also been
found in great numbers on the field of Cannæ in Italy, the
relics of that terrible battle fought between Hannibal and
Æmilius. This tract contains the following passage in reference to Mananan, of which I give a translation from the fourth
volume of the Ossianic Soc. Pub., edited by Mr. Nicholas
O'Kearney,—"The king was thus situated: the race of the
Fomorians imposed a heavy tribute upon the Tuath de Danans
in his reign, a tax was levied upon the growing crops, and an
unga (ingot) of gold was exacted upon the nose of every one
of the Tuath de Danans each year, from Uisneach to Tara
eastward. This tax was to be paid every year, and whosoever

was unable to pay it, his nose was severed from his face. On a certain day Nuadh held a meeting on the Hill of Balar, which is now called Uisneach of Meath. They had not been long assembled there when they discovered a well-appointed host of people approaching them along the plain from the east; and a young man, whose countenance shone like the rising sun, marched at the head of this dense crowd of men. It was impossible to look him in the face, he was so lovely; and he was no other than Luwy the Long-Handed, the sword-exerciser, together with the fairy (enchanted) cavalcade, consisting of the sons of Mananan, his foster-brothers, from Caanan. They had remained but a short time there when they saw an ugly, ill-shaped party of people, namely, nine times nine men, who were the stewards of the Fomorians coming to receive the rents and taxes of the people of Ireland. And with these words Luwy arose, and having unsheathed the sword of *Mananan*, attacked them; and having cut and mangled eight times nine of their number, suffered the remaining nine to put themselves under the protection of the king of Ireland. ' I would kill you,' said Luwy, 'were it not that I prefer you should carry the tidings to the foreigners rather than send my own messengers, lest they might be dishonoured.'"

The Irish mythology, as well as that of the Greeks, is full of reference to weapons endued with supernatural powers: thus the sword of Mananan is frequently introduced in the legendary tales of the ancient Irish. In the volume for 1852 of the *Trans. of the Kil. Arch. Soc.*, p. 32, we have an interesting chapter on folk-lore by Mr. Nicholas O'Kearney, in which he relates a mythic tale of Concovar Mac Nessa, king of Ulster, and of how he became possessed of the magic sword, spear, and shield of Cuillean, or Guillean, a weird smith, or the Vulcan of the the Isle of Man. The passage is as follows: "Cuillean, or Guillean, himself was a very famous being that once resided in Isle of Man, and of so long-lived or mythic a nature as to be found living in all ages of pagan history; at all events

he is represented to have lived at the time when Concovar
Mac Nessa, afterwards king of Ulster, was a young man, who
possessed little prospect of aggrandisements, except what he
might win by his sword. Concovar being of an ambitious and
enterprising nature, consulted the oracle of Cloghor, and was
informed that he should proceed to the Isle of Man, and get
Cuillean, a noted *ceard*, or worker in iron, to make a sword,
spear, and shield for him ; and that the *buadha* (supernatural
power possessed by them) would be instrumental in gaining
him the sovereignty of Ulster. Concovar accordingly repaired
to the Isle of Man, and prevailed on Cuillean to commence the
work ; but while awaiting its completion, he sauntered one
morning along the shore, and in course of his walk met with a
mermaid fast asleep on the beach. Concovar bound the syren,
but she having awoke, and perceiving she was bound, besought
him to liberate her; and to induce him to yield to her petition,
she informed him that she was Teeval, the princess of the
ocean ; and promised, in case he caused Cuillean to form her
representation on the shield, surrounded with this inscription,
' Teeval, princess of the ocean,' it would possess such extraordinary powers that whenever he was about engaging his
enemy in battle, and looked upon her figure on the shield,
read the legend, and invoked her name, his enemies would
diminish in strength, while he and his people would acquire a
proportionate increase in theirs. Concovar had the shield
made according to the advice of Teeval, and on his return to
Ireland such extraordinary success attended his arms that he
won the kingdom of Ulster. The king was not ungrateful, for
he invited Cuillean to settle in Ulster, and bestowed on him
the tract of land along the eastern coast, extending from Glen
Righe, or the Vale of Newry on the Neath, to Glas Neasa on
the river of Annagasson, near Dun-eany on the south, which
were the bounds of the ancient Cooley." This same personage
flourishes in several other mythic tales. He is represented in
the legend of the "Cattle Raid of Cooley" as inviting Concovar

Mac Nessa to visit him at his residence, requesting the king not to bring with him his usual large retinue, excepting a few warriors, because he had no lands or patrimony to support them, relying solely on the produce of his hammer, anvil, and vice.

Mr. O'Kearney further states:—"This same Cuillean, or Guillean, as he is usually styled in popular tradition, resided in a cave on Slieve Gullian, and is still remembered with horror in the traditions of the peasantry; which traditions must have been derived from the notions concerning Guillean, or the form of religion with which he had been connected, inculcated by the first preachers of Christianity. There is in Irish a phrase, 'giolla Guillen;' *i.e.*, the servant of Guillean, synonymous with 'an imp of the Devil,' which strongly warrants this inference." In this there are many points which identify Cuillean with Mananan Mac Lir; first, his intimate connection with the Isle of Man; secondly, his being a forger of supernatural weapons; thirdly, his location in Ulster, where Mananan is said to have reigned over the provincial fairy kingdom; and in the immediate locality where Mananan is stated to have had his fairy palace. Cuillean, too, fell into disrepute among the Christians, as did Mananan.

In that exceedingly curious and mythological tale, the pursuit of Diarmid and Grainne, the particulars of which bear such a startling resemblance to many of the Grecian myths, we have the enchanted weapons of Mananan also introduced. When Diarmid, who answers to the Adonis of the Eastern fable, prepares for the hunt of the wild boar of Ben Gulban, Grainne entreats him to arm himself with the moralltach (sword) of Mananan; but he refuses to do so, and takes with him another weapon: the result is disastrous, and his death ensues. The passage is worth transcribing:—"The day came then with its full light, and he said, 'I will go to seek the hound whose voice I have heard since it is day.' 'Well, then,' said Grainne, 'take with thee the moralltach; that is, the sword

K

130 MANANAN MAC LIR.

of Mananan, and the Ga-dearg (the red spear).' 'I will not,'
said Diarmid; 'but I will take the Beag-alltach (the small
fierce one), and the Ga-buie (yellow javelin) with me in my
hand, and Mac-an-Chuill* by a chain in my other hand.'" . . .
The wild boar then came up the face of the mountain with the
Fenians after him. Diarmid slipped Mac-an-Chuill from his
leash against him, and that profited him nothing; for he did
not wait the wild boar, but fled before him. Diarmid said,
"Woe to him that doeth not the counsel of a good wife; for
Grainne bade me at early morn to-day to take with me the
moralltach and the ga-dearg." Then Diarmid put his small,
white-coloured, ruddy-nailed finger into the silken string of
the ga-buidhe, and made a careful cast at the boar; so that he
smote him in the fair middle of his face, and of his forehead.
Nevertheless, he cut not a single bristle upon him, nor did he
give him wound or scratch. Diarmid's courage was lessened
at that; and thereupon he drew the beag-alltach from the
sheath in which it was kept, and struck a heavy stroke there-
with upon the wild boar's back stoutly, and full bravely. Yet he
cut not a single bristle upon him, but made two pieces of his
sword. Then the wild boar made a furious spring upon Diarmid, so that he tripped him and made him fall headlong. . . .
And when he was fallen to the earth, the boar made an eager,
exceeding mighty spring upon him, and ripped out his bowels
and his entrails, so that they fell about his legs. Howbeit, as
he (the boar) was leaving the Tulach (Hill), Diarmid made a
triumphant cast of the hilt of the sword that remained in his
hand, so that he dashed out his brains and left him dead without life. Therefore, Rath-na-h-Amrann† is the name of the
place that is on the top of the mountain, from that time to
this." The classical scholar will not here fail to observe the
strong resemblance between the death of Adonis and that of
Diarmid. Venus, as we are informed, was enamoured of

* "Mac-an-Chuill" (the son of the hazel), a favourite hound of Diarmid's.
† That is, "The rath of the sword hilt."

Adonis, and used to meet him on Mount Libanus. Mars, envy-
ing his rival, assumed the shape of a wild boar, attacked him
while hunting, gored him with his tusks in the groin, and
killed him. In the Celtic myth, Grainne, the betrothed of
Fion Mac Cumhal, becomes enamoured of Diarmid and elopes
with him; he is pursued from place to place by his vengeful
rival, and at last arrives in the neighbourhood of the mountain
Ben Gulban, where he take up his abode; he goes forth upon
a morning to hunt, when he meets the wild boar (who, as in
the classical legend, is a human being turned into a boar) by
whom he is slain, as above described. Fion, his rival, comes
on the scene while Diarmid is in the agonies of death, who
conjures him (by their former friendship, and by many acts of
assistance and kindness shewn to Fion) to bring him a draught
of water from a certain magic fountain close by, which could
arrest death, and restore Diarmid to his former strength and
vigour. This Fion refuses, and his rival breathes his last. I
shall be excused from digressing so much from the main subject of my paper, but the myth is so full of dramatic interest
and of classical allusions, that I would recommend the perusal
of this very ancient tale to the student of native mythology. It
forms the third volume of the *Ossianic Soc. Pub., Dublin*, 1857.

In an ancient MS., entitled " An T-Octar Gael; or, the
Adventures of Seven Irish Champions in the East", Mananan
is represented as instructing the Celtic hero, Cu-chullin, in the
use of the ga-bolg or sting, which he extracted from a serpent
that infested Loch-na-Nia, near the fort of Mananan in Armenia; this myth would appear to have some bearing on the
use of poisoned weapons among the ancient Irish. In a
very curious and ancient tract, entitled "The Dialogue of
the Sages," and which is found in *The Book of Lismore* (a
vellum MS. compiled in the fourteenth century from more
ancient sources), we have several passages referring to the use
of such deadly arms, from which I extract the following :—
" And valiant Caol-na-Neavan, with a lucky *poisoned* spear

that Finn had, and this was the venom that was on it, for it
never made an erring cast from the hand, and it never wounded
a person when thrown from the hand that would not be dead
before the end of a moment." MS. translation by Mr. Joseph
Long, of Cork.

It is the general opinion of Irish antiquaries that Mananan
Mac Lir was a real personage famous for his exploits as a sea-
rover and coloniser, that he ultimately became deified as the
Irish Neptune, or God of the Sea. It is true, we have him
represented under different names, as Orbsen, Mananan, and
Cuillean; that different attributes and occupations are ascribed
to him. He is sometimes a warrior, a trader, a navigator, a
forger of magic weapons, a potent magician or Druid, so was
also the Grecian deity; he assisted his brother Jupiter in his
military expeditions; he helped Laomedon to build the walls of
Troy; he was a famous ship-builder, and was the inventor of
chariot-races, and had a great variety of names, as Consus,
Enosichthon, Hippius, Soter, etc. Mananan is represented as
enveloping the Isle of Man in mists to protect it from invaders;
—a stratagem, said to have been resorted to by the Tuath-de-
Danans, when the Milesians invaded Ireland. The expelling
of serpents and demons from Ireland is now understood to
signify the overthrow of serpent-worship and other forms of
Paganism which prevailed in that country when Christianity
was introduced. In the historical romance of the " Children
of Lir," we have also a reference to the overthrow of the worship of the Irish sea god. In the myth, the children of Lir
are represented as having been transformed into swans (i.e.,
devoted to the service of the sea god) by their step-mother, a
potent Druidess, and that they remained in this state until the
introduction of the faith, when they were restored to their
natural forms. The following translation of a passage from
this legend will be found in the first volume of the Ossianic
Soc. Pub., p. 101, n. :—" The children of Lir remained in that
condition a long time, until the time of the faith of Christ, and

until Patrick, son of Arpluinn, came into Ireland, and until
Mocomog* came to Inis Gluair of Brendan. And the night
that Mocomog came to the said island, the children of Lir
heard the sound of the matin bell near them. They trembled
violently, and started through excessive dread upon nearing
it. 'What, my dear brothers, has troubled you?' inquired
Fionguala. 'We know not,' replied they, 'canst thou inform
us what that unusual detestable sound which we heard is?' 'It
is the sound of the bell of Mochomog,' replied Fionguala;
'and it is that which will liberate you from suffering, and save
you from adversity with God's will.'"

Angus Oge, or the immortal, was another name for Mananan.
Tradition states that he remained in Ireland until the time of
St. Colomba, that he endeavoured to be reconciled to the
church; but, failing in his efforts, he retired to his original
country, Armenia. This myth evidently points to a struggle
between Paganism and Christianity, which eventuated in the
triumph of the latter.

In vol. 3 of the *Ossianic Soc. Pub.* will be found a curious
romance of the adventures of Cormac Art in the fairy palace
of Mananan; the tale is full of allegory, and represents the
latter as a wise and benevolent being inculcating lessons of
wisdom, and bestowing valuable gifts of a supernatural character on mortals.

This tract is so illustrative of the subject in hand, that I
subjoin the English translation in full:—

"How Cormac Mac Airt got His Branch."

"Of a time that Cormac, the son of Art, the son of Con of
the hundred battles, that is, the arch-king of Erin, was in
Liathdruim, he saw a youth upon the green before his dun,

---

* There were three saints named Mocomog, all disciples of St. Carthogh
of Lismore, who flourished in the seventh century. The personage mentioned above was probably the celebrated St. Mocomog, or Pulcherius, of
Liathmore, who died A.D. 655.

having in his hand a glittering fairy branch, with nine apples
of red gold upon it. And this was the manner of that branch
that, when any one shook it, wounded men, and women with
child, would be lulled to sleep by the sound of the very sweet
fairy music which those apples uttered; and another property
that branch had, that is to say, that no one upon earth would
bear in mind any want, woe, or weariness of soul when that
branch was shaken for him, and whatever evil might have befallen any one, he would not remember it at the shaking of
the branch. Cormac said to the youth, 'Is that branch thine
own.' 'It is indeed mine,' said the youth.' 'Wouldst thou
sell it,' asked Cormac. 'I would sell it,' quoth the youth;
'for I never had any thing that I would not sell.' 'What dost
thou require for it,' said Cormac. 'The award of mine own
mouth,' said the youth. 'That thou shalt receive from me,'
said Cormac, 'and say on thy award.' 'Thy wife, thy son, and
thy daughter,' answered the youth; 'that is to say, Eithne,
Cairbre, and Ailbhe.' 'Thou shalt get them all,' said Cormac.
After that the youth gives up the branch, and Cormac takes
it to his own house to Ailbhe, to Eithne, and to Cairbre.
'That is a fair treasure thou hast,' said Ailbhe. 'No wonder,'
answered Cormac; 'for I gave a good price for it.' 'What
didst thou give for it, or in exchange for it,' asked Ailbhe.
'Cairbre, Eithne, and thyself, O Ailbhe.' 'That is a pity,'
quoth Eithne '(yet it is not true): for we think that there is
not upon the face of the earth that treasure for which thou
wouldst give us.' 'I pledge my word,' said Cormac, 'that I
have given you for this treasure.' Sorrow and heaviness of
heart filled them when they knew that to be true, and Eithne
said, 'it is too hard a bargain (to give) us three, for any
branch in the world.' When Cormac saw that grief and heaviness of heart came upon them, he shakes the branch amongst
them; and when they heard the soft, sweet music of the
branch, they thought no longer upon any evil or care that had
ever befallen them, and they went forth to meet the youth.

'Here,' said Cormac; 'thou hast the price thou didst ask for this branch.' 'Well hast thou fulfilled thy promise,' said the youth, 'and receive (wishes for) victory, and a blessing for the sake of thy truth.' And he left Cormac wishes for life, and health, and he and his company went their ways. Cormac came to his house, and when that news was heard throughout Erin, loud cries of weeping, and of mourning, were made in every quarter of it, and in Liathdruim above all. When Cormac heard the loud cries in Leamhair, he shook the branch among them, so that there was no longer any grief or heaviness of heart upon any one.

"He continued thus for the space of that year, until Cormac said, 'It is a year to-day since my wife, my son, and my daughter were taken from me, and I will follow them by the same path as they took.'

"Then Cormac went forth to look for the way by which he had seen the youth depart, and a dark magical mist rose before him, and he chanced to come upon a wonderful marvellous plain. That plain was thus: there was there a wondrous very great host of horsemen, and the work at which they were was, the covering-in of a house with the feathers of foreign birds; and when they had put covering upon one half of the house, they used to go off to seek birds' feathers for the others; and, as for that half of the house upon which they had put covering, they used not to find a single feather on it when they returned.

"After that Cormac had been a long time gazing at them in this plight, he thus spoke, 'I will no longer gaze at you; for I perceive that you will be toiling at that from the beginning to the end of the world.

"Cormac goes his way, and he was wandering over the plain until he saw a strange, foreign-looking youth walking the plain, and his employment was this: he used to drag a large tree out of the ground, and to break it between the bottom and the top, and he used to make a large fire of it, and to go himself to seek another tree, and when he came back

again he would not find before him a scrap of the first tree that
was not burned, and used up. Cormac was for a great space
gazing upon him in that plight, and at last he said, ' I indeed
will go away from thee henceforth; for were I for ever gazing
upon thee, thou wouldst be so at the end of all.'

" Cormac after that begins to walk the plain, until he saw
three immense wells on the border of the plain, and those wells
were thus: they had three heads in them (*i.e.*, one in each).
Cormac drew near to the well next to him, and the head that
was in that well was thus: a stream was flowing into its mouth,
and two streams were flowing from or out of it. Cormac proceeds to the second well; and the head that was in that well
was thus: a stream was flowing into it, and another stream
flowing out of it. He proceeds to the third well, and the
head that was in that one was thus: three streams were flowing into its mouth, and one stream only flowing out of it.
Great marvel seized Cormac hereupon, and he said, ' I will be
no longer gazing upon you; for I should never find any man
to tell me your histories, and I think that I should find good
sense in your meanings if I understood them.' And the time
of the day was then noon. The King of Erin goes his ways,
and he had not been long walking when he saw a very great
field before him and a house in the middle of the field. And
Cormac drew near the house and entered into it, and the King
of Erin greeted (those that were within). A very tall couple
with clothes of many colours that were within, answered him,
and they bade him stay; ' whoever thou art, O youth; for it
is now no time for thee to be travelling on foot.' Cormac, the
son of Art, sits down hereupon, and he was right glad to get
hospitality for that night.

" ' Rise, O man of the house,' said the woman; ' there is a
fair and comely wanderer by us, and how knowest thou but
that he is some honourable noble of the men of the world, and
if thou hast one kind of food or meat better than another, let
it be brought to me.'

"The youth upon this arose, and he came back to them in this fashion; that is, with a huge wild boar upon his back, and a log in his hand, and he cast down the log and the swine upon the floor, and said, 'There ye have meat, and cook it for yourselves.' 'How should I do that,' asked Cormac. 'I will teach you that,' said the youth; 'that is to say, to split this great log which I have, and to make four pieces of it, and to put down a quarter of the boar and a quarter of a log under it, and to tell a true story, and the quarter of the boar will be cooked.' 'Tell the first story thyself,' said Cormac; 'for the two should fairly tell the story for the one.' 'Thou speakest rightly,' quoth the youth, 'and methinks that thou hast the eloquence of a prince, and I will tell thee a story to begin with. That swine that I brought,' he went on, 'I have but seven pigs of them, and I could feed the world with them; for the pig that is killed of them, you have but to put its bones into the sty again, and it will be found alive upon the morrow.' That story was true, and the quarter of the pig was cooked.

"'Tell thou a story now, O woman of the house!' said the youth. 'I will,' quoth she, 'and do thou put down a quarter of the wild boar, and a quarter of the log under it,' so it was done. 'I have seven white cows,' said she, 'and they fill the seven keives with milk every day, and I give my word that they would give as much milk as would satisfy them to the men of the whole world were they upon the plain drinking it.' The story was true, and the quarter of the pig was therefore cooked. 'If your stories be true,' said Cormac, 'thou indeed art Mananan, and she is your wife, for no one upon the face of the earth possesses those treasures but only Mananan, for it was to Tir Tairrngire he went to seek that woman, and he got those seven cows with her, and he coughed upon them until he learned (the wonderful powers of) their milking, that is to say, that they would fill seven keives at one time.' 'Full wisely hast thou told us that, O youth,' said the man of the house, 'and tell a story

L

for thy own quarter now.' 'I will,' said Cormac,' and do thou lay a quarter of the log under the cauldron until I tell thee a true story.' So it was done, and Cormac said, 'I indeed am upon a search, for it is a year this day that my wife, my son, and my daughters were borne away from me.'' 'Who took them from thee ?' asked the man of the house. 'A youth that came to me,' said Cormac, 'having in his hand a fairy branch, and I conceived a great wish for it, so that I granted him the award of his own mouth for it, and he exacted from me my word to fulfil that; now the award that he pronounced against me was, my wife, my son, and my daughter, to wit, Eithne, Cairbre, and Ailbhe.' 'If what thou sayest be true,' said the man of the house, 'thou indeed art Cormac, son of Art, son of Conn of the Hundred Battles.' 'Truly I am,' quoth Cormac, 'and it is in search of those I am now.' That story was true, and the quarter of the pig was cooked. 'Eat thy meal now,' said the young man. 'I never ate food,' said Cormac, 'having only two people in my company.' 'Wouldst thou eat it with three others, O Cormac,' asked the young man. 'If they were dear to me I would,' said Cormac. The man of the house arose and opened the nearest door of the dwelling, and (went and) brought in the three whom Cormac sought, and then the courage and exultation of Cormac rose.

"After that Mananan came to him in his proper form, and said thus: 'I it was who took those three away from thee, and I it was who gave thee that branch, and it was in order to bring thee to this house that I took them from thee, and there is your meat now and eat food,' said Mananan. 'I would do so,' said Cormac, 'if I could learn the wonders that I have seen to-day.' 'Thou shalt learn them,' said Mananan. 'And I it was that caused thee to go towards them that thou mightest see them. The host of horsemen that appeared to thee covering in the house with birds' feathers, which, according as they had covered half of the house, used to disappear from it, and they seeking birds' feathers for the rest of it—that is a comparison which is applied to poets and to people that seek a fortune, for when they go out, all that they leave behind them in their houses is spent, and so they go on for ever. The young man whom thou sawest kindling the fire, and who used to break the tree between top and bottom, and who used to find it consumed whilst he was away seeking for another tree; what are represented by that, are those who distribute food whilst every one else is being served, they themselves getting it ready, and every one else being enjoying the profit thereof. The wells which thou sawest in which were the heads, that is a comparison which is applied to the three that are in the world. These are they, that is to say :—

" That head which has one stream flowing into it, and one stream flowing out of it, is the man who gives the goods of the world as he gets them.

"That head which thou sawest with one stream flowing into it, and two streams flowing out of it, the meaning of that is the man who gives more than he gets of the goods of the world.

" The head which thou sawest with three streams flowing into its mouth, and one stream flowing out of it, that is the man who gets much and gives little, and he is the worst of the three. And now eat thy meal, O Cormac, said Mananan.

" After that Cormac, Cairbre, Ailbhe, and Eithne sat down, and a table-cloth was spread before them. 'That is a full precious thing before thee, O Cormac,' said Mananan, 'for there is no food, however delicate, that shall be demanded of it, but it shall be had without doubt.' 'That is well,' quoth Cormac. After that, Mananan thrust his hand into his girdle and brought out a goblet and set it upon his palm. 'It is one of the virtues of this cup,' said Mananan, ' that when a false story is told before it, it makes four pieces of it, and when a true story is related before it, it will be whole again.' ' Let that be proved,' said Cormac. 'It shall be done,' said Mananan. ' This woman that I took from thee she has had another husband since I brought her with me.'

Then there were four pieces made of the goblet. · 'That is a falsehood,' said the wife of Mananan. 'I say that they have not seen woman or man since they left thee, but their three selves.' That story was true, and the goblet was joined together again. 'Those are very precious things that thou hast, O Mananan,' said Cormac. 'They would be good for thee to have,' said Mananan. 'Therefore they shall all three be thine, to wit, the goblet, the branch, and the table-cloth, in consideration of thy walk, and of thy journey this day; and eat thy meal now, for were there a host and a multitude by thee thou shouldst find no scarcity in this place. And I greet you kindly as many as you are, for it was I that worked magic upon you, so that ye might be with me to night in friendship.'

" He eats his meal after that, and that meal was good, for they thought not of any meat, but they got it upon the table-cloth, nor of any drink, but they got it in the cup, and they returned great thanks for that to Mananan. Howbeit, when they had eaten their meal, that is to say, Cormac, Eithne, Ailbhe, and Cairbre, a couch was prepared for them, and they went to slumber and sweet sleep, and where they rose upon the morrow was in the pleasant Liathdruim, with their table-cloth, their cup, and their branch. Thus far then the wandering of Cormac, and how he got his branch." (*Publications of the Ossianic Soc.*, v. iii.)

Many other notices of Mananan Mac Lir will be found scattered through the pages of Irish legendary lore.

N.B.—It is stated in the above Memoir that the Isle of Man derived its name from " Mananan Mac Lir". It appears, however, to be more correct to say that he got his name from the island with which he was so intimately connected. For we must remember that there was an other Mona or Man, with which he had no connection whatever, viz., Anglesea.
· · It has been observed in the first volume of the Manx Society, page 140, that the two Monas most probably derived their name from their reputed holy character, as the "Sedes Druidarum", the abode of the *Holy Wise Men*, and that the name has the same connection with the Sanscrit root, Mán, in reference to religious knowledge, as our word Monk; so also Moonshee and the names of ancient lawgivers, as Manu, son of Brahma, Menu, Minos, and Menes. (Editor, J. G. C.)